As one of the world's longest established
and best-known travel brands,
Thomas Cook are the experts in travel.

For more than 135 years our
guidebooks have unlocked the secrets
of destinations around the world,
sharing with travellers a wealth of
experience and a passion for travel.

**Rely on Thomas Cook as your
travelling companion on your next trip
and benefit from our unique heritage.**

Thomas Cook **pocket** guides

TALLINN

Thomas
Cook

Your travelling companion since 1873

Researched by Scott Diel & Riina Sepp
Updated by Riina Sepp

Published by Thomas Cook Publishing
A division of Thomas Cook Tour Operations Limited
Company registration No: 3772199 England
The Thomas Cook Business Park, 9 Coningsby Road
Peterborough PE3 8SB, United Kingdom
Email: books@thomascook.com, Tel: +44 (0)1733 416477
www.thomascookpublishing.com

Produced by The Content Works Ltd
Aston Court, Kingsmead Business Park, Frederick Place
High Wycombe, Bucks HP11 1LA
www.thecontentworks.com

Series design based on an original concept by Studio 183 Limited

ISBN: 978-1-84848-283-8

First edition © 2006 Thomas Cook Publishing
This third edition © 2009 Thomas Cook Publishing
Text © Thomas Cook Publishing
Maps © Thomas Cook Publishing/PCGraphics (UK) Limited
Transport map © Communicarta Limited

Series Editor: Lucy Armstrong
Project Editor: Linda Bass
Production/DTP: Steven Collins

Printed and bound in Spain by GraphyCems

Cover photography (Medieval armour in Tallinn) © Simon Reddy/Alamy

CONTENTS

SYMBOLS KEY

The following symbols are used throughout this book:

@ address ☎ telephone ⓦ website address ⓛ opening times
ⓝ public transport connections ❶ important

The following symbols are used on the maps:

i	information office	▪	points of interest
✈	airport	O	city
✚	hospital	O	large town
ⓥ	police station	○	small town
⊟	bus station	═	motorway
⊟	railway station	▬	main road
✝	cathedral	▬	minor road
❶	numbers denote featured	▬	railway
	cafés & restaurants		

Hotels and restaurants are graded by approximate price as follows:
£ budget price **££** mid-range price **£££** expensive

Abbreviations used in addresses:
mnt.   maantee (road)
pst.   puiestee (avenue)
tn.   tänav (street)

❍ *Church spires, domes and towers add to Tallinn's enchanting skyline*

INTRODUCING
Tallinn

Introduction

The main reason why the capital of Estonia is such a compelling city to visit right now is that it's at a key point in its evolution. In the last 20 years, the country has experienced a traumatic (if much-welcomed) rupture from Soviet-style communism and has embraced the values of Western-style democratic capitalism. A new country is being born, and the place in which you can most clearly witness the effects of its spectacular evolution is, of course, Tallinn.

But that's just the main reason; there are many others, and not the least of these is the city's proportions, which you might describe as small but intriguingly formed. More petite than, say, Riga and Vilnius, Tallinn can largely be covered on foot. A lot is packed into the city, and most of the major points of interest are within 2 km (1¼ miles) of the centre of town. Add to this clean air, clean streets, little traffic congestion and warm and friendly residents; add to that the architectural and cultural heritage created by a thousand years of eventful history and you can see exactly why tourists are waking up to the good news that is Tallinn. However, the city recognises that as it's been forced to hide its attractions under a bushel for so long, it cannot allow cost to prohibit potential visitors from becoming actual ones. Thus it is a comparatively inexpensive destination in which to have a thoroughly good time.

Whatever your area of interest – stunning medieval architecture, fabulously uninhibited nightlife, beautifully unspoilt areas of greenery or the chance to see the remnants of Soviet culture while you still can – Tallinn offers the lot. The city will always be fascinating, but why not treat yourself to a visit now, at this particularly vivid moment in its history?

● *It's not just church roofs that look attractive in the Old Town*

When to go

Tallinn's climate is not one of extremes, and most of the year the weather is amenable. If you don't like the cold, February is the month to avoid; if you don't like it hot you can visit Tallinn at any time of year. October to February can be rather dark months, which limits time for sightseeing, although the darkened, snow-filled city, with warm fireplaces in medieval settings, offers a charm of its own that attracts more and more people every winter.

SEASONS & CLIMATE

Tallinn's climate is controlled by incoming streams of warm water from the Atlantic Ocean, moderated by the Baltic Sea. This gives the city a moderate, maritime climate, with summers not too hot, and winters not too cold. The humidity in summer can be high, up to 80 per cent. Thus, Tallinn tends to be rather cloudy and damp, with an average of about 500 mm (19.5 in) of precipitation a year.

Spring starts in mid-April, and comes in quickly, with an explosion of green in the fields, and multicoloured flowers just about everywhere. July and August, although the warmest months, are also the wettest, with frequent showers. Mid-summer temperatures average 16°C (60°F) and can reach more than 30°C (86°F). Autumn is long and warm.

Winter gets serious in November, and lasts until April, with snow usually on the ground from late December until late March. Winter temperatures average -5°C (23°F) and rarely go over 4°C (39°F). April and October tend to be unpredictable, with both cold, wintry days

● *There's more than a chance of snow early in the year*

and warm, spring-like days. May, June and September are the most comfortable months in which to visit.

But visiting Tallinn at any time of year is rewarding, the run-up to Christmas being especially pleasant.

ANNUAL EVENTS

The summer solstice is the holiday that Estonians anticipate most keenly. The entire country takes time off to revel in the long day of light. Summer days in general are enthusiastically celebrated, with all kinds of music and dance festivals that embrace national and international cultures. It's the time for medieval markets, beer fests and, happily, nights of barely restrained hedonism.

Late autumn and winter don't mean a slowdown in activity for the city: film festivals, concerts and dances simply move indoors.

In December the Tallinn Christmas Market returns to Raekoja Plats (Town Hall Square). A gigantic Christmas tree is the centrepiece of the fair, surrounded by huts selling everything from handicrafts to food. Live performers entertain, and, of course, there's that visit from Santa.

January–February
Baroque Musique Festival A week-long festival of baroque music showcasing Estonian performers and musicians from all over the world. ❶ 614 7760 Ⓦ www.concert.ee

April
Estonian Music Days This festival, held in venues around town, is devoted to new music based on classical Estonian works.
❶ 645 4068, 646 6536 Ⓦ www.helilooja.ee
Jazzkaar One of Tallinn's best-attended events, this international

jazz festival, which takes place in venues all across the city, mixes traditional and cutting-edge music. Organising body the Jazzkaar Friends Society holds other jazz events throughout the year.
📞 611 4405 🌐 www.jazzkaar.ee

June
Celebration of St John's Day Bonfires, dancing, music, games and legends are all part of the mid-summer festival celebrating the longest day of the year. 📍 Estonian Open-air Museum (see page 94)
📞 654 9100 🌐 www.evm.ee

Old Town Days Every year for four days in the summer, Town Hall Square (see page 75) is turned into a medieval market overflowing with goods, handicrafts and art. Scattered within the confines of the Old Town you'll find people playing the parts of tradesmen, nobles, jesters and musicians. 🌐 www.vanalinnapaevad.ee

Getting medieval in Tallinn for the Old Town Days festival

July

Medieval Market In the Old Town, traditional trade folk bring their skills to life while others – almost certainly the same ones who honoured last month's Old Town Days with their presence – dress up in period clothing. ❶ 660 4772 Ⓦ www.folkart.ee

Õllesummer The biggest beer fest in the Baltic comes to Tallinn for five days every summer. Drink deep while listening to rock, reggae, blues, jazz and Estonian music. ❸ Lauluväljak (Song Festival Grounds, see page 96) Ⓦ www.ollesummer.ee

August

August Dance Festival A lively international festival of dancing, highlighting emerging new artists. Events are held mainly at the Kanuti Gildi Saal venue in the Old Town. ❸ Pikk 20 ❶ 646 4704 Ⓦ www.saal.ee

Birgitta Festival Opera, ballet and musical performances in the ruins of Pirita convent ❶ 669 9947 Ⓦ www.birgitta.ee

October

International New Music Festival (NYYD) A festival of contemporary music, with around a hundred new works. Held every odd-numbered year at venues all over the city. ❶ 614 7760 Ⓦ www.concert.ee

November–December

Pimedate Ööde Filmifestival (Tallinn Black Nights Film Festival) This combines showings of both professionally produced feature-length films and the works of students. ❶ 631 4640 Ⓦ www.poff.ee

Christmas Jazz Music to cheer the darkest nights kicks off in late November and continues in various venues throughout December.
🕿 611 4405 🌐 www.jazzkaar.ee

Christmas Market Town Hall Square in the Old Town comes alive with the sights and sounds of Christmas every day until 6 January. A huge Christmas tree is the showpiece, surrounded by huts selling crafts, food, ornaments and toys.
🌐 www.christmas.ee

PUBLIC HOLIDAYS
New Year's Day 1 Jan
Independence Day 24 Feb
Good Friday 2 Apr 2010, 22 Apr 2011, 6 Apr 2012
Easter Sunday 4 Apr 2010, 24 Apr 2011, 8 Apr 2012
Spring Day 1 May
Whit Sunday 23 May 2010, 12 June 2011, 27 May 2012
Victory Day 23 June
St John's Day 24 June
Day of Restoration of Independence 20 Aug
Christmas Eve 24 Dec
Christmas Day 25 Dec
Second Day of Christmas 26 Dec

E-stonia: totally wired

Estonia's youthful population are as e-sazzy as any in Europe –
perhaps even more so. The country's ardent embrace of the internet
has caused a societal revolution which has, in its own way, been
every bit as consequential as the political upheaval that culminated
in the country's independence in 1991.

In fact, internet communication was key to the success of the
revolutionary movement in the late 1980s (see page 21): student
activists, who were hip to the then-new technology, used email to
organise protests and meetings, setting up internet points in the
countryside around Tallinn to frustrate government snooping. This
is why even the most remote rural outposts are fully connected
today. As soon as the authorities realised what was going on, they
established their own net-surveillance infrastructure, which was
subsequently used as the foundation for Estonia's post-independence
technological big bang; and what a big big bang it's been.

Today, even old grannies in Estonia have mobile phones, and almost everyone uses the internet on a regular basis. It's an astonishing progression when you consider that, less than 20 years ago, hot water was regarded as a luxury in a lot of places outside Tallinn. Having such good access to the internet and technology can only be a good thing for the country's future development.

Wireless technology has entered daily life. Estonia's health service monitors people with conditions such as hypertension and diabetes via tiny devices that are inserted into the body and transmit data to healthcare teams. Ironically, the formerly secretive and repressive processes of government have become remarkably open, thanks to e-governance: papers and documents are freely available on the web, and the country has pioneered online voting. Elections since 2005 have been carried out using this medium, without running into problems with either the technology or the possibility of corruption.

Estonia is confident and progressive with most information technology

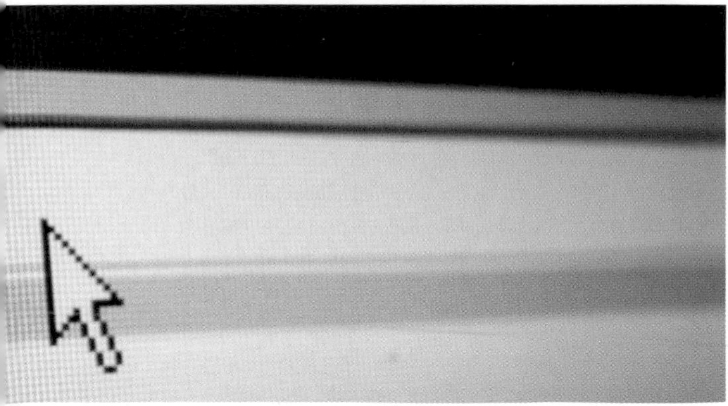

History

Due to its strategic location between Eastern and Western Europe, Tallinn has a long and varied history: the vast periods of occupation that Estonia has endured makes its current independence all the more important.

The area around Tallinn was first settled 3,500 years ago by Finno-Ugric migrants. The settlement slowly grew, and by the tenth century it was an important trading city for Scandinavian and Russian merchants. By the mid-12th century, Tallinn was appearing on world maps.

Next, German 'Knights of the Sword' arrived, bringing with them Christianity and Western European culture. Then, in 1219, Tallinn was conquered by the Danes. The city acquired its current name – from *Taani linn* ('Danish city') – during this period, which also saw the development of *Toompea* ('Dome hill') and its cathedral, and the imposition of the street network that still exists today. In 1285, Tallinn joined the Hanseatic League.

In 1346, Denmark sold Northern Estonia, including Tallinn, to Germany. For the next 200 years (a period known as the 'Golden Age'), Tallinn flourished, and grew into one of the biggest and most powerful towns in Northern Europe, fortified with 66 defensive towers.

The Reformation of 1524 replaced the cultural influence of the Catholic Church with that of the Lutheran, which began school education for the citizens. The Livonian War, a three-party affair between Russia, Poland and Sweden, with Estonia caught in the middle, ended the Golden Age and, in 1561, the Swedes captured Tallinn, although it was another 65 years before all of Estonia fell under Swedish rule. This era was referred to as 'The Good Old Swedish Times', surely ironically, as Tallinn spent it languishing economically. Falling into Russian hands in the Northern War in 1710 was not such a disaster as one might think: the Tsars allowed Tallinn a fair amount of autonomy, and started building it into an important Russian port, as well as developing it as an industrial city.

After World War I and the Russian Revolution, Estonia declared itself independent on 24 February 1918, but it took two years of fighting against both Germany and Russia before the country's independence was recognised by the Tartu Peace Treaty on 2 February 1920. This brief blossom of independence ended with World War II, when first Russia, then Germany, and then Russia once more occupied Estonia.

With the fall of Soviet Russia (signalled by the 'Singing Revolution', see page 21), Estonia once again declared independence on 20 August 1991. The country joined NATO in March 2004 and then the European Union in May of the same year. Since then, Estonia has taken an active – sometimes vigorous – part in EU affairs. The final accolade – admission to the euro – is expected in 2013. Tallinn itself is managing its rapid development into a modern city with dash and brio.

⊙ *Tallinn's citizens are now free to celebrate their culture*

Lifestyle

What a difference a decade or so makes: only 20 years ago you would find people having to queue for such necessities as toothpaste and tomatoes. Now there are major department stores and shopping centres, expensive cars parked on cobble-stoned streets and a population that's more than happy to welcome a flood of visitors.

Estonians may seem a somewhat shy people until they get to know you. In terms of how you should approach them initially, a good rule is to be friendly, but never over-familiar. They are, really, fun-loving and outgoing. You'll observe their exuberance in the café and bar scene that is a huge part of everyday Estonian life; expect thought-provoking dialogues from well-educated locals in the cafés during the day and lively party scenes in the clubs and pubs at night. Tallinn seems to hold more (and longer) festivals than any other country in the Baltics.

Estonians are remarkably high-tech. They are avid users of the internet and lap up new technology – thus the nickname 'E-stonia'

THE GOOD GUEST'S GUIDE
Estonians can be a little shy, so don't take it personally if you attend a party and no-one offers their hand. Younger Estonians have more quickly adopted this Western custom, but older ones have not. If you're invited into someone's home, count yourself lucky, as this has great meaning in a culture where most people simply keep to themselves. When entering someone's home, always remove your shoes (since streets in Tallinn used to be dirty, it is considered a courtesy to remove footwear). It is generally the custom for guests to bring flowers.

(see page 14). Technology aside, if you ask an Estonian his or her idea of a good time, the reply might well be 'a walk in the woods' or 'a day spent fishing'. For all their urban lifestyle and Wi-Fi technology, Estonians are naturalists at heart.

⬥ *Alfresco cafés have sprung up all around the city*

Culture

Tallinn cannot rival metropolises like London or New York in size or international standing, but it doesn't let that stand in its way. Live theatre, opera, symphony, folk music, choirs, art, newspapers, magazines and, of course, the dialogues in the coffee houses are

● *The Song Festival Grounds celebrate a key facet of Estonian life*

THE SINGING REVOLUTION

Song festivals have played a massive role in Baltic life since the 19th century, when the rediscovery of folk songs started to rejuvenate the indigenous cultures that had been weakened by centuries of foreign domination. During the Soviet period, singing festivals were the only expression of national solidarity that were tolerated.

In 1988, the labour unions and the Estonian Heritage Society organised a massive Song Festival at the Lauluväljak (Song Festival Grounds) in Tallinn (see page 96). The festival became the focus of mass demonstrations against the Soviet regime. This movement became known as the 'Singing Revolution', and the term was used to describe the independence movement in all three Baltic States – Estonia, Latvia and Lithuania.

Perhaps the greatest demonstration of inter-Baltic solidarity occurred on 23 August 1989, when two million people joined hands to form a human chain stretching from Tallinn to Vilnius. Song festivals are still held, and still pack a potent emotional punch, now that independence is well assured.

all parts of Estonia's complex, lively, and ever-evolving cultural scene. Since Estonia regained its independence with the fall of the Soviet Union, cultural life has begun a rapid evolution, embracing all kinds of new media and virtual art. Yet it continues to hold dear its traditions. The Song and Dance Festival takes place in Tallinn every five years in July (2014, 2019) beginning with a festive parade of performers to the Song Festival Grounds in Pirita (see page 96 & Ⓦ www.laulupidu.ee for details).

Music is a major part of Estonian life, and both the National Symphony Orchestra and National Opera have earned solid reputations worldwide. Aside from the traditional concert hall venues of the Great and Small Guilds, the Old Town has a plethora of atmospheric sites for music, including medieval churches.

Music is more than just a part of the Estonian culture, however: it is the frame that holds the tapestry of culture in this country. The tradition of folk music is centuries old, and Estonia boasts one of the largest collections of folk songs in the world, with written records of some 133,000 songs. It is no wonder that the country's break from the Soviets came with the 'Singing Revolution'.

Live theatre is another favourite pastime of Tallinn residents. From the traditional **Estonian Drama Theatre** (Ⓐ Pärnu mnt. 5 Ⓣ 680 5555 Ⓦ www.draamateater.ee) to the cutting-edge presentations of the **Salong-Theatre** (Ⓦ www.salong-teater.ee) and **Theatre NO99** (Ⓐ Sakala 3 Ⓣ 660 5051 Ⓦ www.no99.ee), Estonians appear to embrace drama in all its forms. Youngsters are introduced to live theatre at the Estonian Puppet Theatre (see page 148). A truly avant-garde experience is the **Von Krahl Theatre** (Ⓐ Rataskaevu 10 Ⓣ 626 9090 Ⓦ www.vonkrahl.ee), which performs in a cabaret-like hall.

Estonians are also avid readers, and they like to keep themselves well informed. The Tallinn Central Library, which opened in 1907 and has more than 20 branches (for a city of less than 500,000 people), is one of the oldest in Estonia.

◗ *The colourful clock face of the Church of the Holy Ghost*

MAKING THE MOST OF
Tallinn

Shopping

If you last visited Tallinn when the Soviets were in charge, you're in for a surprise: the shopping scene has changed exponentially, and the city certainly doesn't lack for any number of places to spend your money these days. The Old Town (see page 68) is filled with dozens of souvenir, antiques, clothing and speciality shops.

The most popular souvenir items are knitted goods like sweaters and mittens, patchwork quilts, trinkets bearing the city name, and spirits. For a truly authentic Estonian souvenir, purchase a Kihnu Island sweater (see below). The main shopping streets in the Old Town are Viru, Müürivahe, Suur-Karja, plus Kullassepa near Town Hall Square.

You'll also find craftsmen plying their wares along Müürivahe in the Old Town. Their prices are sometimes cheaper, and the

KIHNU ISLAND SWEATERS

Kihnu is an island off Estonia's western coast which has a long history of producing beautiful knitwear. These beautiful, warm sweaters are unique in design (often blue-and-white or black-and-white) with decorative collars, and make ideal souvenirs or presents. The best place to buy one is from the charming old women who man the stands on Müürivahe Street near the Viru Gate. Bargaining is usually fruitless, unless you're planning on purchasing larger quantities.

▶ *Medieval fairs are a marketplace for traditional crafts and foodstuffs*

USEFUL SHOPPING PHRASES

What time do the shops open/close?
Mis kell kauplused avatakse/suletakse?
Mis kell kah-up-lused ahvah-tahk-se/su-letahk-se?

How much is this?
Kui palju see maksab?
Kuy pal-yu se-eh mak-sab?

Can I try this on?
Kas ma tohin seda proovida?
Kas mah toh-hin seh-da pro-o-vi-da?

My size is ...
Minu number on . . .
Mi-nuh nub-ber on . . .

I'll take this one, thank you
Aitäh, ma võtan selle
Ay-tahh, mah vo-tan sel-leh

Can you show me the one in the window/this one?
Näidake mulle palun seda vaateaknalt/seda?
Nay-da-keh mul-leh pah-loon seh-da vah-ah-te-ahk-nalt/seh-da?

This is too large/too small/too expensive
See on liiga suur/liiga väike/liiga kallis
Se-eh on lee-ga su-ur/lee-ga vay-keh/lee-ga kal-lis

salespeople (generally older women) even more charming than most you'll meet in the shops.

At the other end of the retail scale, you'll find plucky, small-scale entrepreneurs hawking postcards outside nearly every tourist attraction. A flea market near the Old Town can turn up such lovely finds as a pure linen poncho or leather goods, and if you feel that a Russian-made fur hat would set you off, this is a good place to look.

Stockmann and Tallinna Kaubamaja (see page 88), the two largest department stores in town, sell everything you could desire, from clothing and cosmetics to electronics. These locations are your best bet for any item you left at home.

Don't overlook the shopping centres, which can be glitzy and airy. The newest is Viru Keskus (see page 88), which contains the largest bookshop in the Baltics as well as the usual stores. The **Kristiine Centre** (🅐 Endla 45 🆆 www.kristiinekeskus.ee), meanwhile, has clothing, grocery and speciality stores all in one place. For upmarket chic in the Old Town, try the smaller **Demini Centre** (🅐 Viru 1), which is a good place to purchase handicrafts to take home.

Probably the tourists' most popular purchase is amber, and you'll find countless places to buy this Baltic treasure. But telling real from fake requires deft application of a flame – plastic melts, amber doesn't – and it's a person of rare personal charm who can get away with starting a fire in a foreign shop.

Eating & drinking

Estonian cuisine is rich in meat, potatoes and dairy products, with pork, cheese and sour cream involved in some manner with almost every dish. Rye bread, salted herring and beer are also traditional foods.

A traditional Estonian starter is *sült*, a mixture of pork pieces set in jelly. It is an acquired taste. Most restaurants feature salted herring, smoked eel and sliced sausage, all served with delicious dark rye bread, as a starter.

Soup can be either a starter or a snack for lunch. The most common soup is *seljanka*, a Russian broth of meat, pickled vegetables and fish. Other light meals include *pelmeenid* (akin to Italian ravioli), *pirukad* (dough stuffed with bacon and cabbage) and pancakes with cheese, meat or mushrooms. Salads are becoming more common. You may want to try a traditional Estonian salad of peas and pickles served in sour cream. Plates of greens, often laced with tuna, are also a local favourite.

The standard Estonian main course is pork with potatoes and *sauerkraut*. The pork comes either as roast, or as a chop in batter. It usually has a good rind of fat which, when properly cooked, is delicious. Other meat courses, based on beef, chicken and blood

PRICE CATEGORIES

The restaurant price guides used in this book indicate the approximate cost of a three-course meal for one person, excluding drinks.

£ up to 60kr. ££ 60–150kr. £££ over 150kr.

⬤ *Tallinn's cafés and bars range from traditional to downright trendy*

sausage, are common, as are pan-fried freshwater fish such as trout, perch and pike.

Vegetarians shouldn't despair, although their options may be somewhat limited. A few exclusively vegetarian restaurants have opened, but, sadly, all of them failed. Tallinn's restaurants, though, are becoming more used to vegetarian customers and generally have something on the menu. The best bet is to head to other ethnic eateries. As Tallinn becomes more cosmopolitan, a much wider variety of ethnic foods from around the world is becoming available, with French, Italian, Greek, Indian, Japanese and Chinese restaurants, to name a few, already well established.

Estonians love their sweets. The most common dessert is *mannapuder* (semolina pudding), often served with fruits and berries. Pancakes filled with jam are another local favourite. Cakes, flans, tarts and cheesecake are widely available.

On the liquid side, the Estonians prefer coffee or soft drinks in the daytime, and beer in the evening. (They customarily take their coffee black: if you want cream or sugar, you will have to ask for it.) Espresso and cappuccino are available, but filter coffee is most common in restaurants where large numbers of tourists are served. Locals often accompany their coffee with a sticky bun or piece of cake.

There is an increasing number of bars and pubs in Tallinn, most in the English and American style. The beer normally comes as a regular lager, and the locals consume a lot of it. Stronger beers and ales are also available. Beer is normally sold by the half-litre (that's nearly a pint), and ordering lesser amounts is frowned upon. A traditional Estonian spirit is *Vana Tallinn*. A rather syrupy and medicinal liqueur, it is easier to drink watered down with fruit juice or coffee; some find it quite tasty mixed with champagne. Thanks to the Russian influence, good vodka is also readily available, and at good prices.

Restoran, meaning restaurant, indicates a more upmarket establishment, complete with menus and table service. There are many of these in Tallinn, including in most major hotels. For something more informal, try a café, where you order and pay at the counter. Many pubs and bars also offer a full menu.

With Tallinn's abundance of green spaces and parks, especially adjacent to the Old Town, you should try a picnic in the park one sunny afternoon.

USEFUL DINING PHRASES

I would like a table for ... people
Ma soovin lauda ... inimesele
Mah so-ov-in lau-da ...ih-ni-meh-seh-leh

Waiter/waitress!	**May I have the bill, please?**
Kelner! Ettekandja!	Ma palun arve?
Kelner! Ettekandyah!	*Mah pah-loon ar-veh?*

Could I have it well-cooked/medium/rare please?
Palun praadige liha tugevalt/keskmiselt/pooltooreks?
*Pah-loon pra-a-di-ghe ly-hah tuh-ghe-valt/kesk-mi-selt/
poh-ohl-toh-oh-reks?*

I am a vegetarian.	**Where is the toilet**
Does this contain meat?	**(restroom) please?**
Ma olen taimetoitlane.	Palun, kus asub WC?
Kas see sisaldab liha?	*Pah-loon, kus a-sup*
Mah olen tayme-toytlane.	*veh-tseh?*
Kahs se-eh see-sahl-dahb liha?	

I would like a cup of/two cups of/another coffee/tea
Ma palun ühe tassi/kaks tassi/veel kohvi/teed
Mah pah-loon u-heh tas-si/kaks tas-si/ve-el koh-vi/te-ed

I would like a beer/two beers, please
Palun üks õlu/kaks õlut
Pah-loon uks oh-lyuh/kaks oh-lyuht

31

Entertainment & nightlife

Don't be surprised that a small city can have such a variety of nightlife and after-hours entertainment available. Tallinn seems capable of accommodating almost every taste, from the ear-splitting rock of a packed nightclub to the quiet sophistication of a cigar and brandy lounge.

Most of the nightlife is in and around Tallinn's Old Town. You won't need to make plans to visit a specific club; simply wander from place to place until you find one that suits your style. Some are just metres apart from each other.

Timing is everything. Friday is the night to party in Tallinn. Thursdays and Saturdays are also quite lively, but the rest of the week can be almost dull by comparison to Friday. During the week the bars are usually open only until midnight and some clubs don't even bother to open on a Sunday, Monday or Tuesday.

Tallinn's cultural life outside the bar is also wide and varied. The National Symphony and National Opera are two stalwarts that can be counted on for quality performances. You'll also discover that the small venues of the Old Town include churches that offer medieval and Early Music performances. Chamber music concerts are frequently held in the House of the Blackheads.

Theatre is not to be overlooked in the city, although most of the performances will be in Estonian. If you can spend an evening enthralled in stage craft, you'll not want to miss the chance of attending a play or two.

A live performance of music will transcend any language barriers, and Tallinn boasts no shortage of concerts and performances. Yes, you'll find lots of classical and operatic music, but Tallinn is heavily into jazz, pop and all kinds of contemporary sounds. For tickets and listings information, see Ⓦ www.piletilevi.ee or visit the Piletilevi office in Viru Keskus shopping centre (see page 88).

Need your entertainment on a big screen? Tallinn hosts the Black Nights Film Festival (see page 12) in November and December. During the rest of the year, many multiplex theatres show both mainstream and art films, many in English with Estonian subtitles. The **Coca-Cola Plaza** (Ⓐ Hobujaama 5) and **Kosmos** (Ⓐ Pärnu mnt. 45 Ⓦ www.forumcinemas.ee) feature mostly Hollywood fare; try the **Sõprus** (Ⓐ Vana-Posti 8 Ⓣ 644 1919 Ⓦ www.kino.ee) or **Kinomaja** (Ⓐ Uus 3 Ⓣ 646 4068 Ⓦ www.kinomaja.ee) for more avant-garde selections.

🔺 *Tallinn has many live music performances*

Sport & relaxation

SPECTATOR SPORTS

Basketball and football are the two most popular spectator sports in Estonia, with the latter enjoying a definite vogue as the national team gets better and better.

Basketball, hockey and other sports take place in the Saku Suurhall Arena (see page 86). Football matches are held at **A Le Coq Arena** (ⓔ Asula 4c), which is about a thirty-minute walk southwest of the city centre.

Horse racing, especially trotting with sulkies (two-wheeled carts), is popular in Tallinn. Racing takes place at the **Tallinn Hippodrome** (ⓐ Paldiski mnt. 50 ⓣ 677 1677 ⓦ www.hipodroom.ee ⓝ Trolleybus: 6, 7; bus: 21).

PARTICIPATION SPORTS

In the summer months, Estonians take to the great outdoors, with hiking, canoeing, cycling and birdwatching popular activities. Most of this is done well outside Tallinn in places such as Lahemaa National Park (see page 135), **Soomaa National Park** (ⓦ www.soomaa.com), or along the many kilometres of Baltic coastline. These areas have

WINTER SPORTS

With the long winters, skiing is popular in Estonia. The best skiing is cross-country, as there are few hills high enough for a good downhill run. Otepää, in southern Estonia, is the leading ski resort. Estonia came second on the medals table of the 2006 Winter Olympics.

well-maintained hiking trails and nature paths. Deer, moose and elk are commonly sighted along these trails, as are the occasional bear and wild boar.

Exercise and fitness are big in Estonia. Some major hotels feature exercise facilities and swimming pools. If you want to jog, stick to Pirita and Kadriorg, as other areas of the city are dimly lit, and have many dogs on the loose. Tallinn has several clubs that offer aerobics, weightlifting and yoga, and many have swimming pools and saunas.

Facilities for basketball, billiards, bowling, cycling, horse riding, ice skating, swimming, skating, squash and tennis are also available in the city – the tourist office can provide details (see page 153).

RELAXATION

Most of Estonia takes the month of August off to go to summer houses in the countryside. If you should happen not to get an invitation, there are plenty of spas in and around Tallinn where relaxation is guaranteed (see page 136).

◆ *Estonia is a great place for skiing*

Accommodation

New hotels are springing up like daisies to accommodate the ever-growing tourist demand. As a rule of thumb, the most luxurious establishments are located in the Old Town area, with more economical choices found in the city centre and in the suburbs. Some of the budget hotels are products of the Soviet era and are not likely to have been renovated. Hotels, especially in summer, should be booked months in advance.

As there is no public transport within the Old Town (see page 64), the best way to reach hotels located in this area is by taxi if you have heavy luggage, or by foot if you don't.

HOTELS

Dzingel ££ A large, somewhat remodelled Soviet hotel in Tallinn's Nõmme garden district, outside the city areas covered in this guide. It has all the services you'd expect at a Western hotel, though it's a bit worn around the edges. ⓐ Männiku tee 89 ⓣ 610 5201 ⓦ www.dzingel.ee ⓝ Bus: 5

Hotel G9 ££ Located on the third floor of a Stalinist-era office building, this is a simple hotel with very basic services (but an excellent

---

PRICE CATEGORIES

The ratings below indicate the approximate cost of a room for two people for one night.

£ under 600kr.   ££ 600–900kr.   £££ 900–1500kr.
£££+ over 1500kr.

kebab restaurant). The price is right and the city-centre location fab.
ⓐ Gonsiori 9 (City Centre) ⓣ 626 7130 or 626 7131 ⓦ www.hotelg9.ee
ⓝ Bus: 1A, 5, 8, 34A, 38, 51, 60, 63

Domina Inn City ££–£££ An elegant hotel tucked into the Old Town.
The influence is clearly Italian, with light marble floors and sweeping
staircases. ⓐ Vana-Posti 11/13 (The Old Town) ⓣ 681 3900
ⓦ www.dominahotels.com

Romeo Family Hotel ££–£££ A family-run hotel in the Old Town that
offers a level of personal service that's hard to beat – if you get past
the language barrier. The breakfast area, like the rooms, has a cosy
atmosphere. ⓐ Suur-Karja 18, 4th floor, Apt. 38 (The Old Town)
ⓣ 644 4255

Stroomi ££–£££ A great hotel just yards from the beach and ten
minutes' drive west of the city centre. It rents out bicycles and
roller skates as well. ⓐ Randla 11 ⓣ 630 4200 ⓦ www.stroomi.ee
ⓝ Bus: 40, 48

Uniquestay Mihkli ££–£££ The cheaper sister hotel of the Von
Stackelberg Hotel has clean, Scandinavian design and flat-screen
computers in every room. Good value for money. ⓐ Endla 23 (The
Old Town) ⓣ 666 4800 ⓦ www.uniquestay.com

Old Town Maestro's £££ A six-storey boutique hotel in the heart
of the Old Town's night scene that features art deco-influenced
interiors and spacious rooms. ⓐ Suur-Karja 10 (The Old Town)
ⓣ 626 2000 ⓦ www.maestrohotel.ee

Pirita Cloister Guesthouse £££ Run by the nuns of the St Bridgettine Order, this is not recommended for those who want to party; but for those who want a quiet night's sleep, it's perfect. Located in the cloister in the Tallinn suburb of Pirita. ❷ Merivälja tee 18 (Suburbs East & West) ❶ 605 5000 ❿ www.piritaklooster.ee ⓝ Bus: 1A

St Barbara £££ This hotel doesn't boast much in the way of frills but the rooms are comfortable and the location is great, in the City Centre

△ *Reputedly the tallest building in Estonia – the Radisson hotel*

but right near the Old Town. If you need to stay connected, there's a computer in the lobby for guest use. Ⓐ Roosikrantsi 2a (City Centre) ⓘ 640 0040 Ⓦ www.stbarbara.ee Ⓝ Tram: 3, 4

Scandic Palace £££ Part of the Scandic international hotel chain, so expect a good room. It is well situated in the City Centre, close to the Old Town. Ⓐ Vabaduse väljak 3 (City Centre) ⓘ 640 7300 Ⓦ www.scandic-hotels.ee Ⓝ Tram: 3, 4

Villa Hortensia £££ A guesthouse in a recently renovated Old Town master's courtyard and a pleasantly unusual find. The hotel shares its location with a gallery and artisans' workshops, which attracts an artistic clientele. As there is no reception at the guesthouse, you need to phone ahead for the keys. Ⓐ Vene 6 (The Old Town) ⓘ 504 6113 Ⓦ www.hoov.ee

L'Ermitage £££–£££+ Small and traditional, this is a wonderful place to hide away. The rooms have lots of creature comforts such as internet connection and flat-screen TVs. It's also clean, efficient and downright friendly. Centrally located in the Old Town, just west of Toompea Hill. Ⓐ Toompuiestee 19 (The Old Town) ⓘ 699 6400 Ⓦ www.lermitagehotel.ee

Radisson Blu Hotel Tallinn £££–£££+ You shouldn't have any difficulties finding a room in what is said to be the tallest building in the country. It's a business hotel, with health club and sauna, and the location is good for both Old Town and the city centre. The views from the roof-top bar are stunning. Children under 12 stay for free. Ⓐ Rävala 3 (City Centre) ⓘ 682 3000 Ⓦ www.radissonblu.com Ⓝ Trolleybus: 1, 3, 6

Baltic Hotel Vana Wiru £££+ With its spacious rooms with satellite TV, marbled floors and Wi-Fi in the lobby, this Old Town hotel is living proof that traditional can seamlessly blend with techno. ❷ Viru 11 (The Old Town) ❶ 669 1500 ❿ www.vanawiru.ee

Hotel Schlössle £££+ Truly a medieval setting. Heavy wooden beams, massive stone fireplaces and wrought-iron chandeliers are just a few of the touches that give this small hotel its baronial ambience. If the view doesn't sweep you off your feet, the price might. ❷ Pühavaimu 13/15 (The Old Town) ❶ 699 7700 ❿ www.schlossle-hotels.com

Hotel St Petersbourg £££+ Dating back to 1850, this is Tallinn's oldest continuously functioning hotel. The interiors are amazing, and the staff are great. The location is hard to beat, too: very close to the epicentre of the Old Town, with everything within easy reach. ❷ Rataskaevu 7 (The Old Town) ❶ 628 6500 ❿ www.schlossle-hotels.com

Kolm Õde £££+ An outstanding boutique hotel located inside three of the best-known medieval buildings in Estonia. Known locally as the Three Sisters, the buildings look as though they have stepped straight out of a fairy tale. Inside, the hotel offers comfort in very stylish, individually designed rooms ❷ Pikk 71/ Tolli 2 (The Old Town) ❶ 630 6300 ❿ www.threesistershotel.com

Meriton Old Town Hotel £££+ A nice hotel on the edge of the Old Town. The rooms are somewhat small but cheerful in décor. The lobby contains part of the old city wall and the round outer edge of the neighbouring 15th-century mill. ❷ Lai 49 (The Old Town) ❶ 614 1300 ❿ www.meritonhotels.com

🔺 *Kolm Õde in the fairytale Three Sisters*

● Indulge yourself in the pool and spa at the Telegraaf hotel

Telegraaf £££+ Located in Tallinn's old telegraph station, this 5-star hotel is the only one in the Old Town with underground parking. An Elemis spa, swimming pool and Wi-Fi in every room make this hotel a favourite of those travelling on expense accounts. ⓐ Vene 9 (The Old Town) ⓣ 600 0600 ⓦ www.telegraafhotel.com

The Von Stackelberg Hotel £££+ A well-planned central hotel that has everything you might want, including a computer in each room. The cosy café/restaurant in the basement is worth visiting even if you're not staying in the hotel. ⓐ Toompuiestee 23 (The Old Town) ⓣ 660 0700 ⓦ www.uniquestay.com

HOSTELS

City Bike Hostel £ Located on a charming street on the edge of the Old Town, City Bike offers excellent room rates, but can also organise bicycle travel and tours to just about anywhere in Estonia. ⓐ Uus 33 (The Old Town) ⓣ 511 1819 ⓦ www.citybike.ee

Eurohostel £ Near Town Hall Square, this is an excellent Old Town choice for backpackers and budget travellers. The interiors are simple and there are both double rooms and dorms that sleep four to six people. ⓐ Nunne 2 (The Old Town) ⓣ 644 7788 ⓦ www.eurohostel.ee

Tallinn Backpackers £ A hostel that always scores high for camaraderie, a bonus for people travelling alone. It offers free use of the sauna and kitchen. ⓐ Olevimägi 11 (The Old Town) ⓣ 644 0298 ⓦ www.tallinnbackpackers.com

THE BEST OF TALLINN

TOP 10 ATTRACTIONS

- **Toompea Castle** Sitting at the very top of Toompea Hill, Toompea Castle stands as a sentry that for most of Tallinn's history has guarded the city. It is dominated by three defensive towers, the tallest of which, 'Tall Herman', dates from 1371 and proudly flies the Estonian flag (see page 76)

- **St Nicholas's Church** Begun in the 13th century, and rebuilt in the 15th century, this imposing church is now a museum for Tallinn's collection of medieval art (see page 74)

- **Kadriorg Park** This beautiful park, containing a palace that houses the Museum of Foreign Art, was built by Tsar Peter the Great (see page 92)

- **Raekoda & Raekoja plats (Town Hall & Town Hall Square)** As old as Tallinn itself and surrounded by medieval buildings painted in pastel colours, the square is a popular rallying point for Estonian patriotism (see page 75)

- **Alexander Nevsky Cathedral** Built in 1900, this onion-domed Russian Orthodox Church can be seen from most parts of the city (see page 68)

- **Great Sea Gate** At the very northern end of the Old Town, the Great Sea Gate is a 16th-century arch flanked by two towers. The larger of the two towers is called Fat Margaret (see page 76)

- **House of the Blackheads** The Brotherhood of the Blackheads was a merchants' guild founded in 1343, and the house was built to accommodate visiting businessmen. The house is elaborately decorated in Renaissance style, both inside and out (see page 73)

- **Botanic Gardens** Located in Pirita, the gardens feature a large area dedicated to virtually every type of tree and plant found in Estonia, and then some (see page 96)

- **Estonian Open-air Museum** Located on the western outskirts of Tallinn, this is an ethnographic collection of over a hundred 18th- and 19th-century buildings uprooted from around Estonia and brought to this one spot (see page 94)

- **Church of the Holy Ghost** Built in the 1360s, this is the only church in Tallinn whose exterior remains in its original form (see page 74)

🔽 *Find a good vantage point for an aerial view of the city*

Suggested itineraries

HALF-DAY: TALLINN IN A HURRY

If your time for sightseeing is limited to only a few hours, you're in luck as many of the city's top attractions are bunched quite close together. There is no logical way to wander the streets, so use Raekoja plats (Town Hall Square, see page 75) as a hub and take side trips out and back.

First, explore Town Hall Square. There are two buildings of interest: the Town Hall to the south, and the Town Hall Pharmacy to the north. Behind the Town Hall is the Museum of Photography (see page 80). There are also lots of coffee shops and souvenir stands here. Just a few steps south of the square is the Tourist Office, where you can pick up a map of the city.

The first excursion will be to Toompea. This is the toughest part of the trip, as it features a steep climb. Going west out of the Square, you come to Pikk Street. Continue west until you reach the gate tower once used to keep the local peasants out of Toompea. Go through the gate and climb up along Pikk Jalg Street. At the top you come to Alexander Nevsky Cathedral (see page 68). Walk round the cathedral to find Toompea Castle (see page 76). Then walk north along Toom-Kooli until you come to Kiriku plats, with the Lutheran Cathedral, **Püha Neitsi Maarja Piiskoplik Toomkogudus** (Cathedral of Saint Mary the Virgin, also known as the Dome Church ❸ Toom-Kooli 6 ❶ 644 4140 ⓦ www.eelk.ee/tallinna.toom). Take one of the streets on either side of the museum, and you will come to a lookout on the top of the wall that gives a good view of the harbour and the Old Town. Now, retrace your steps to Town Hall Square.

The second trip will take you north. Next to the Town Hall Pharmacy is a small alley (Saiakang) that leads to the Church of the Holy Ghost (see page 74). Northwest of the Church is Pikk Street, and here you will find the House of the Great Guild, which contains the Estonian History Museum (see page 79). Continue northeast on Pikk for the House of the Blackheads (see page 73), Oleviste Kirik (St Olaf's Church, see page 74), the Three Sisters and, finally, the Great Sea Gate and the Maritime Museum (see pages 76 & 79).

Start to retrace your steps, but turn right at the Three Sisters (Tolli Street), and then left on Lai Street. Here you will see high-gabled merchants' houses, then turn right on Suur-Kloostri Street to find the Church of the Transfiguration (see page 70). Turn left on Väike-Kloostri Street for a good look at the remnants of the city wall, then left on Nunne Street until you come to the gate tower, and then head back to Town Hall Square.

The third trip takes you south from Town Hall Square along Kullassepa Street to St Nicholas's Church (see page 74). West of the church is Lühike Jalg Street, which heads up to the Adamson-Eric Museum (see page 79). Walking south and east will take you to the **Eesti Teatri-ja Muusikamuuseum** (Estonian Theatre & Music Museum ⓐ Müürivahe 12 ⓣ 644 6407 ⓦ www.tmm.ee ⓛ 10.00–18.00 Wed–Sat. Admission charge). Return to Town Hall Square via Harju Street.

1 DAY: TIME TO SEE A LITTLE MORE

Once you've visited all the Old Town sights, then you can venture into the suburbs of Tallinn. The three trips listed below should each take about three-quarters of a day.

Top of the list would be Kadriorg Park (see page 92), which is about 1 km (½ mile) due east of the Old Town. On the way, stop at the A H Tammsaare Muuseum at Koidula 12a (see page 88). Once you are in the Kadriorg Park grounds, see the **Eduard Vilde Muuseum** (ⓐ Roheline Aas 3 ⓣ 601 3181 ⓦ www.linnamuuseum.ee/vilde),

Kadriorg Palace (see page 92), Peter the Great's House and the ornamental garden. Just outside the park are the Song Festival Grounds (see page 96).

A second trip takes you about 2 or 3 km (1¼–2 miles) east of the Old Town and into Pirita. First you will encounter Maarjamäe Loss (Maarjamäe Palace), which now houses part of the Estonian History Museum (see page 79). In Pirita itself, you will find a huge yachting marina, Pirita Beach and the Botanic Gardens (see page 96). Be sure to visit the observation platform on the television tower for a great view of Tallinn.

A third trip takes you west to the upmarket suburb of Rocca al Mare, about 6 km (3½ miles) west of the Old Town. Here you will find Tallinn Zoo (see page 147) and the Estonian Open-air Museum (see page 94).

HERE COME THE STAG WEEKENDERS

With relatively inexpensive flights from London to Tallinn, an increasing number of young British men are flocking to Tallinn for weekend stag parties. Tour companies specialising in this type of entertainment lure them with promises of good, clean and cheap merriment.

These vivacious fun-lovers show up as groups of modern-day ratpackers, flitting from pub to pub like butterflies and generally whooping it up. Favourite spots of these wandering bands of young men include Molly Malones on the square and almost any of the larger bars on Viru or Suur-Karja Streets. Long live the stag weekenders, and long may they enliven Friday and Saturday nights.

Serious art fans should not miss **Kumu** (ⓐ Weizenbergi 34/Valge 1
ⓘ 602 6000 ⓦ www.ekm.ee ⓥ Tram: 1, 3; bus: 31, 67, 68), Estonia's
national art museum, which opened in 2006. The museum is cut
into a limestone cliff and seems to serve as a bridge between
historic Tallinn (beneath) and Soviet Tallinn (above).

2–3 DAYS: TIME TO SEE MUCH MORE

If you have several days, you may want to explore the surrounding
countryside. Lahemaa National Park (see page 135) is about an hour's
drive (70 km/43 miles) east of Tallinn and has a full range of facilities
and accommodation. As well as many well-marked hiking and
nature trails, there are beach resorts and even a couple of restored
palaces.

LONGER: ENJOYING TALLINN TO THE FULL

Once you've explored the city, head out west or south. Although
a car is the best way to get around, all places described here have
regular bus services from Tallinn.

If you want a few days at a beach resort, then Pärnu, 'Estonia's
Summer Capital', is the only place to go (see page 100). The city has
a 7 km (4½ mile) beach, which is packed with sunbathers in July and
August.

For unspoiled landscape you should travel to the Estonian
Islands in the Baltic, namely Vormsi, Hiiumaa, Saaremaa and Muhu.
The islands are sparsely populated, accommodation is minimal,
and local public transport is non-existent. Plan on taking a car, and,
if going in summer, make sure you have reserved accommodation.

For the intellectually inclined, a day or two in Tartu (see page 116)
is a must.

Something for nothing

Visit the Old Town and spend an hour or two wandering the steep streets of the medieval core of the city. Marvel at the construction of the buildings that has allowed them not only to last the centuries but also to adapt to new uses such as art galleries and cafés.

Tallinna Kunstihoone (City Gallery ⓐ Harju 13 ⓘ 644 2818 ⓦ www.kunstihoone.ee ⓛ 12.00–18.00 Wed–Sun) is noted for its frequently changing contemporary and experimental exhibitions. Best of all, it's free. Draakoni Gallery (Dragon's Gallery, see page 81) holds small exhibitions of local and international artists in its beautiful Old Town location which is decorated with dragons carved from stone. In the **Eesti Rahvusraamatukogu** (National Library of Estonia ⓐ Tõnismägi 2 ⓘ 630 7611 ⓦ www.nlib.ee ⓛ 12.00–18.00 Mon–Fri, summer; 11.00–20.00 Mon–Fri, 12.00–19.00 Sat, winter ⓝ Trolleybus: 1, 2, 3, 6) you'll find lots of reading matter, but there's also a permanent exhibition of graphic artist Eduard Wiiralt's work. The Soviet architecture itself is interesting. The Tallinn Art Hall Foundation (see page 86) has some very daring art inside the conservative walls of its 1930s building. The smaller exhibition in the Hall is always free, but the main gallery can be seen at no charge on the last day of each temporary show.

For a free experience, you can't beat a fair or a festival. In the summer months the Old Town's streets come to life, especially during the Old Town Days and Medieval Market festivals (see pages 11 & 12), when you'll find locals dressing up in period costume.

▶ It costs nothing to browse the Medieval Market

When it rains

If the weather is not wonderful, do as the Estonians do and head for a café to drink coffee and discuss how to solve the problems of the world. Then, once you have had your caffeine fix, you'll have plenty of energy to explore some of the city's museums.

Start with the Linnamuuseum (Tallinn City Museum, see page 80), located in a handsomely restored merchant's house. From medieval costumed figures to posters and photographs, this museum brings the history of Tallinn to life. A bonus is that much of the explanatory text is in English.

Directly across the street from the City Museum is the Dominican Monastery (see page 70), once one of the most powerful institutions in medieval Tallinn. Today, it is home to a comprehensive collection of medieval and Renaissance stone carvings, including some very intricately carved tombstones.

Still need to burn off some of that caffeine? Head to the **Energia Keskus** (Energy Centre ❸ Põhja pst. 29, near the harbour ❶ 715 2650 Ⓦ www.energiakeskus.ee ❶ 10.00–18.00 Mon–Fri, 12.00–17.00 Sat) for some hands-on experiences with technology. This museum is filled with some strange-looking machinery that may leave you wondering about its purpose as not all signs have been translated into English.

If the weather is not only rainy but cold, spend some time in a sauna. Although Estonia's neighbour to the north, Finland, reigns undisputed as the sauna capital of the world, Tallinn does have its fair share of hotspots. There's even a medieval 'Sauna Tower' in Tallinn's Old Town. A lot of hotels and sports clubs in Tallinn have saunas available to rent by the hour. At **Kalma** (ⓐ Vana-Kalamaja 9a ❶ 627 1811 Ⓦ www.bma.ee/kalma ❶ 10.00–23.00), the oldest public bath in Tallinn, a sauna may be taken for between 95–130kr. If you want a more upmarket sweat, try the **Meriton Grand Hotel** (❸ Toom pst. 27 ❶ 667 7100) at 900kr. per hour in the evening. Should you drink beer as part of the sauna experience? By all means after you've finished, but not before. Alternatively, take yourself off to one of the day spas in Tallinn or nearby Pirita.

Note that a spa visit in Estonia can involve a bit of pampering, but it may also reveal the true state of your health. If you're not keen to confront that reality, opt for a soothing massage instead.

◆ *There are some hot and steamy venues when it's cold outside*

On arrival

TIME DIFFERENCE

Estonia is two hours ahead of Greenwich Mean Time (GMT), and three hours ahead during daylight saving time between the end of March and the end of October.

ARRIVING

By air

Tallinn Lennart Meri Airport (ⓐ Lennujaama tee 2 ⓣ 605 8888 ⓦ www.tallinn-airport.ee) is small, uncrowded and was renovated in 2009. It is located just 3 km (2 miles) from the city centre and has excellent facilities, including ATMs, currency exchange, duty free shops, restaurants and tourist information. Car rental companies are on the ground floor, next to the entrance to the car park.

To reach the city, take bus 2, which leaves every 20 minutes (every 30 minutes on Sundays) between 07.00 and 00.00. It runs between the airport, the city centre and the port and costs 20kr. Tickets can be purchased directly from the bus driver. A taxi from the airport to the city centre should cost about 120kr.

By rail

There are regular train services from Moscow in Russia. Local services run to Tartu, Viljandi and Pärnu, but train travel is not a hugely popular form of transport in Estonia.

The train station is situated near the Old Town and is about 1 km (½ mile) from both the city centre and the harbour. There are currency exchange booths in the train station and ATMs next to the front doors. From the train station to the city centre, take trams 1 or 2, or just walk a couple of hundred metres into the Old Town.

Balti Jaam Train Station ⓐ Toompuiestee 37 ⓣ 1447 (within Estonia)
ⓜ Tram: 1, 2; trolleybus: 4, 5, 7; bus: 21, 21B, 59

By road
Tallinn is connected by international bus lines to most major cities
in Latvia, Lithuania, Russia, Poland and Germany.

Tallinn Central Bus Station (ⓐ Lastekodu 46 ⓣ 12550 (within
Estonia) ⓜ Tram: 2, 4; bus: 2, 15, 39) is located 1 km (½ mile) from
the city centre. There is a cash-only currency exchange at the terminal,
but its rates are poor. There is an ATM by the main entrance.

Most incoming buses stop at more central locations, such as
Viru väljak, before reaching the main terminal. From the bus station
to other parts of the city, take trams 2 or 4, or buses 17, 17A or 23.
A taxi to the Old Town should cost about 50kr.

Tallinn is connected to the rest of Europe by two major highways:
Highway 1 (E20) goes east to Russia, and Highway 4 (E67) goes

ⓥ *The train from Moscow*

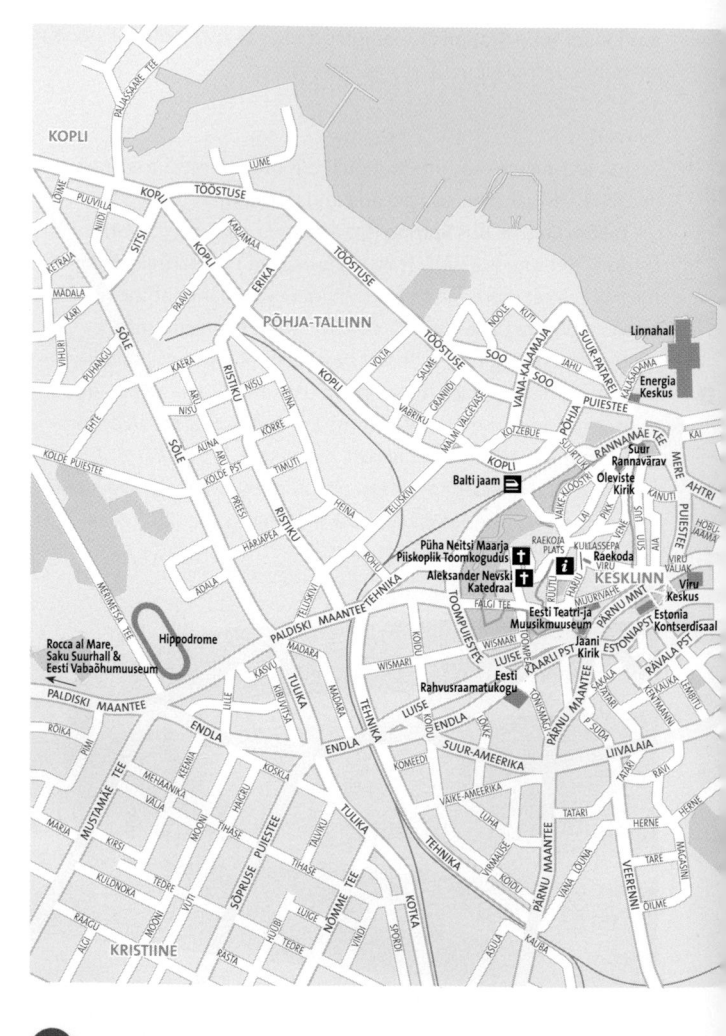

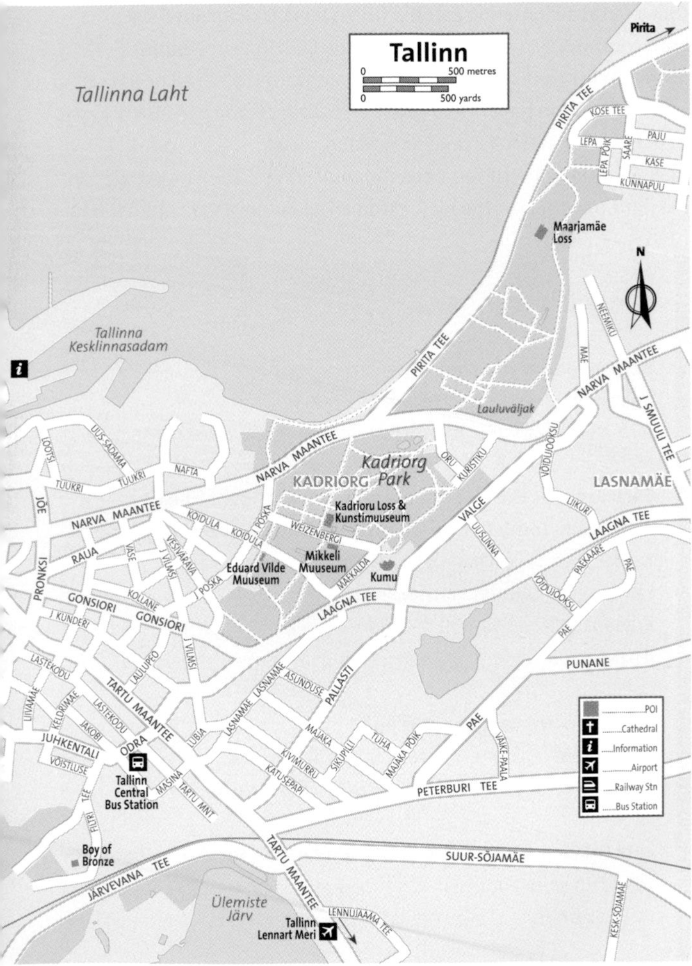

Tallinn

0 ————— 500 metres
0 ————— 500 yards

Pirita

Tallinna Laht

PIRITA TEE
KOSE TEE
LEPA PÕIK
PAJU
SAARE
KASE
KÜNNAPUU

Maarjamäe
Loss

N

Tallinna
Kesklinnasadam

PIRITA TEE

NEEMEKI

MÄE

NARVA MAANTEE

J. SMUULI TEE

Lauluväljak

LASNAMÄE

NARVA MAANTEE

LOOTSI
TUUKRI
TUUKRI
NAFTA
KOIDULA
KOIDULA
POSKA

Kadriorg
Park

KADRIORG

ORU
KURISTIKU

VÕIDUJOOKSU

UKURI

LAAGNA TEE

JÕE
NARVA MAANTEE

Kadrioru Loss &
Kunstimuuseum

WEIZENBERGI

VALGE

UUSLINNA

PRONKSI
RAUA

VESIVÄRAVA
J. VILMSI
KÕLLANE

POSKA

VILMSI

Eduard Vilde
Muuseum

Mikkeli
Muuseum

Kumu

MÄEKALDA

LAAGNA TEE

VÕIDUJOOKSU

PAE

GONSIORI
KUNDERI

GONSIORI

LAULUPEO

LASNAMÄE
LASNAMÄE
ASUNDUSE

PALLASTI

PAE

VÄIKE-PAALA

PUNANE

LASTEKODU
LIIVAMÄE
PELGRANNA
JAGOBI

LASTEKODU

TARTU MAANTEE

VIISU

MAJAKA

KIVIMURRU

TUHA

MAJAKA PÕIK

SOMPA

KATUSEPAPI

JUHKENTALI
VÕISTLUSE

ODRA

MÄGISE TARTU MNT.

Tallinn
Central
Bus Station

Boy of
Bronze

JÄRVEVANA TEE

TARTU MAANTEE

PETERBURI TEE

SUUR-SÕJAMÄE

KESK-SÕJAMÄE

POI
Cathedral
Information
Airport
Railway Stn
Bus Station

Ülemiste
Järv

Tallinn
Lennart Meri

LENNUJAAMA TEE

south to Latvia. Entering Estonia from Latvia is quite easy, since both countries are now members of the EU. However, entering from Russia can take a bit of time. In both cases, you will need the car's registration papers and proof of insurance. You can also bring a car in by ferry from Finland or Sweden.

In Estonia, as in the rest of continental Europe, the traffic drives on the right-hand side of the road. Estonian law requires an international

---

IF YOU GET LOST, TRY...

Excuse me, do you speak English?
Vabandage, kas te oskate inglise keelt?
Vah-ban-da-ghe, kas teh os-kah-teh ing-li-seh ke-elt?

Excuse me, is this the right way to the Old Town/the city centre/the tourist office/the station/the bus station?
Kuidas minna vanalinna/kesklinna/turismiinfosse/
raudteejaama/bussijaama?
Kuy-das minnah va-nah-lee-nah/kesk-lee-nah/toor-eess-meen-fosser/rowd-te-eh-ya-a-mah/pussy-ya-a-mah?

Can you point to it on my map?
Kas te võite näidata, kus see on kaardi peal?
Kas teh voy-teh nay-da-tah, kus se-e on ka-ar-di pe-al?

I am looking for this address
Ma otsin seda aadressi
Mah ot-sin seh-da a-ad-res-sy

I am looking for the . . . hotel
Palun, kus on hotell . . .
Pah-loon, kus on hot-tel . . .

---

driver's licence and a valid insurance policy. During daylight hours, dipped headlights or daytime running lights must be used. After dark, the main headlights must be switched on. The driver and the passengers must wear seat belts at all times. Petrol stations are easy to find. The largest international chains operating in Estonia are Statoil and Neste.

Both major highways take you right to the centre of town. Traffic is light compared to many cities, so driving into town is easy.

Parking in the city centre and the Old Town area must be paid for, although the first 15 minutes of parking are free. A valid parking ticket must be displayed in your windscreen from 07.00–19.00 on weekdays and 08.00–15.00 on Saturdays in the city centre. In the Old Town, parking must be paid for 24 hours a day. Tickets are sold by special guards. Guarded and indoor car parks are also available.

By water

Ferries and catamarans arrive from Finland and Sweden at the passenger port, which is less than 1 km (½ mile) from the centre of town and has currency exchange booths and ATMs. A taxi from the port to the centre of town should cost about 40kr.

Bus no. 2 will take you into town. The cost is 20kr. and tickets are available from the driver. A taxi from the port to the centre of town should cost about 70kr.

FINDING YOUR FEET

Traffic in Tallinn is light compared to other large cities, but the driving tends to be aggressive and definitely not pedestrian friendly. Foreign visitors are especially vulnerable and should take extra precautions at intersections.

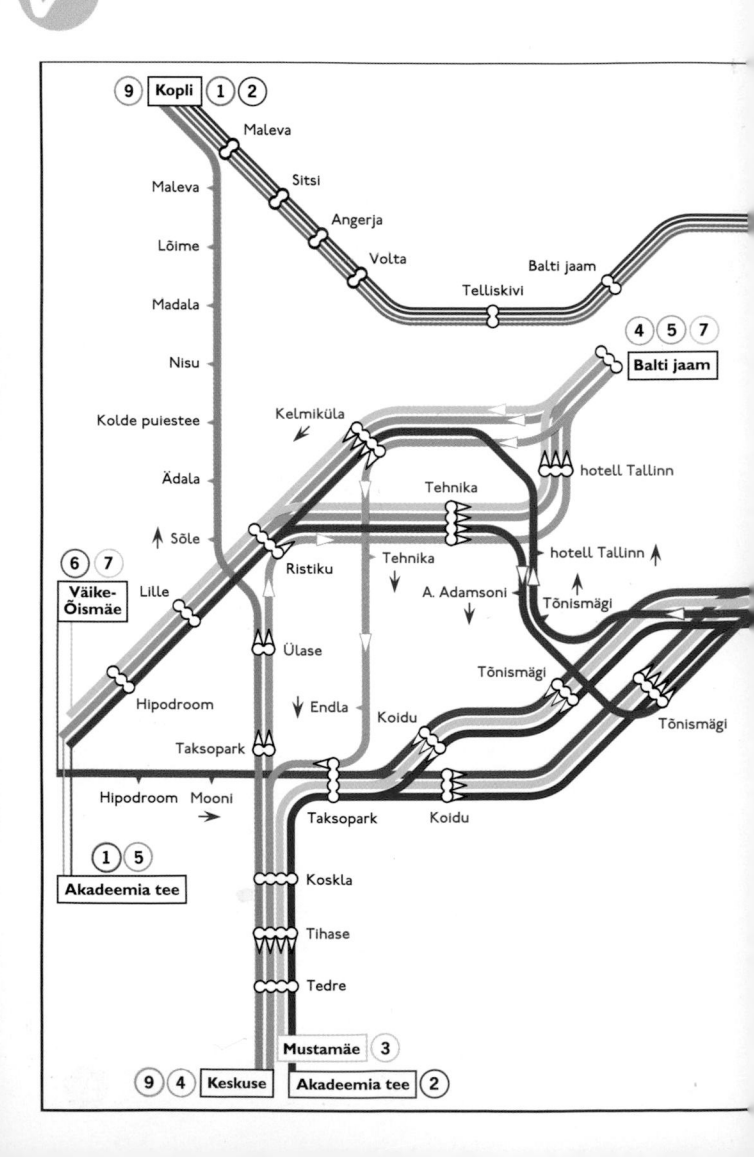

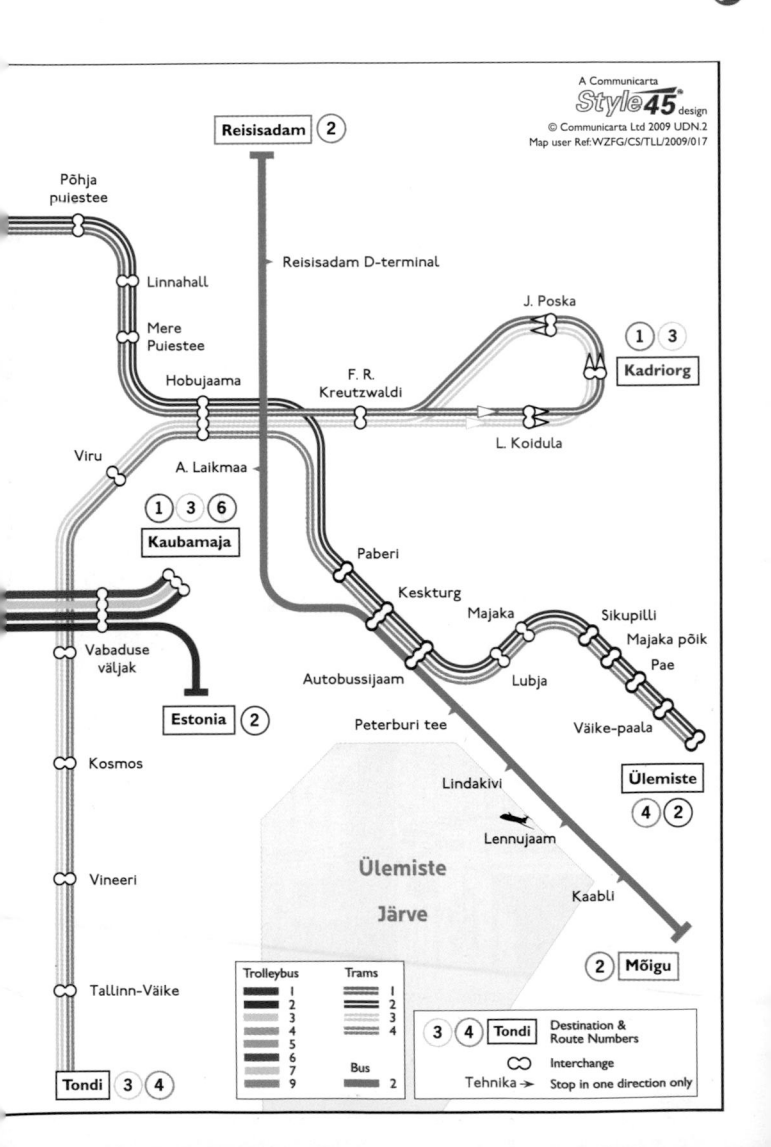

Although the overall crime rate is low, petty theft is a problem, especially from cars. Stealing from hotel rooms, especially the cheaper ones, is not uncommon. Sneak thieves and pickpockets are less prevalent than in Western European cities, but do represent a problem. Visitors would be well advised not to carry large sums of cash, and not to flaunt expensive jewellery, cameras or electronic equipment. Such items are better left at home unless really needed. Tallinn also has its share of muggers, so beware of areas that are not well lit, or derelict in appearance, especially at night and near drinking establishments. If possible, do not walk alone.

● *Tallinn's city centre is compact and quaint*

The exception to normal city life is the Old Town. Here, the narrow winding streets are not conducive to cars, and few are present, with the exception of early morning hours when the Old Town is full of aggressive delivery drivers. With most of the Old Town reserved for pedestrians, everything seems to run at a much more leisurely and relaxed pace.

English is quite commonly spoken in Estonia, and more and more Estonians, especially those in international business and the tourist industry, are learning it. There is one English-language newspaper in Estonia: the *Baltic Times* is published weekly and is available at most hotels, some restaurants and many news-stands. Other English-language publications are shipped into Tallinn, and again, are available at most major hotels, and at many news-stands.

ORIENTATION

Tallinn sits on a bay in the Gulf of Finland, about 85 km (53 miles) south of Helsinki. The historic heart of Tallinn, the Old Town, is 1.2 km (just under a mile) long by about 1 km ($^1/_2$ mile) wide. It sits on a hill overlooking the bay, and for the most part is surrounded by defensive walls built in medieval times.

The skyline of the Old Town is dominated by the spires of several churches and the turrets of Toompea Castle. Raekoja plats (Town Hall Square) is virtually in the geographic centre of the Old Town. The streets of the Old Town radiate outwards from Town Hall Square in a rather haphazard fashion.

The rest of the 'new' city radiates eastward and westward from the Old Town. A few kilometres east is the suburb of Pirita (see page 96), while about 6 km ($3^1/_2$ miles) west is the upmarket suburb of Rocca al Mare, home to the Estonian Open-air Museum (see page 94).

Toompea, which is built on the top of the hill that dominates Tallinn, is the main city landmark, and easily seen from anywhere in the city. If you get lost, just head for the hill to get your bearings.

GETTING AROUND

Tallinn is a fairly small, compact city, so getting around is quite easy. The centre of the city is Viru väljak. It is at the foot of the hill, or dome, upon which Toompea and the Old Town are built, and is also the junction of Highway 1 (Narva maantee) from the east, and Highway 4 (Pärnu maantee) from the south.

Many of the points of interest are within 1 km (½ mile) of Viru väljak, and most are within 2 km (1¼ miles). As the city is so pedestrian-friendly, walking is the best way to see certain parts of it, which is why some addresses in this guide have no public transport information.

To reach destinations outside the Old Town, you can hop on one of the buses, trams or trolleybuses. They're cheap, efficient and easy to use. The best deal in town is a Tallinn Card (available for 6, 24, 48 or 72 hours, ranging from 185–495kr.), which, for a reasonable price, allows you unlimited use of public transport as well as free or discounted access to many museums and attractions. Cards are available from the tourist office (see page 153).

The main railway station is at the northwest foot of the Old Town, and a short 200 m (660 ft) walk, albeit uphill, puts you inside the Old Town. The main bus terminal is about 1 km (½ mile) southeast of the Old Town, with regular local bus services directly to the Old Town and surrounding areas.

Taxis are also available, but be warned that some drivers are less than scrupulous. Make sure that the taxi has a visible meter, that it works, and that the driver starts it. The driver should also have his registration, complete with photograph and stamps, prominently

◐ *Trams are another way of getting around in Tallinn*

displayed. The cost of a taxi from one point to another within the city centre should be no more than 120kr. It is always a good idea to ask your driver for a receipt. If you suspect you were dealt with dishonestly, your hotel receptionist can check your receipt to make sure the distance travelled matches your fare. Quality hotels have clout with the taxi companies, and over-charged passengers can and do receive refunds.

CAR HIRE

Unless you are going to visit locations outside Tallinn, renting a car is not recommended. The city is compact enough, with most of the attractions close enough, that walking, using the public transport, or even hiring taxis, is much more economical and practical. Also, parking spaces are hard to find, and expensive. Most of the major car rental agencies are represented either at the airport, or in the city centre, or both. You can expect to pay the same prices as in Western Europe. There are some local car rental companies that can be cheaper than the major ones, but the mechanical condition of the car may be questionable.

Some major car rental agencies are:

Avis ⓐ Pärnu mnt. 141 ❶ 667 1500 ⓒ 08.00–17.00 Mon–Fri
ⓦ www.avis.ee

Budget ⓐ Tallinn Airport ❶ 605 8600 ⓒ 09.00–18.00
ⓦ www.budget.ee

Europcar ⓐ Tallinn Airport ❶ 605 8031 ⓒ 09.00–18.00
ⓦ www.europcar.ee

Hertz ⓐ Tallinn Airport ❶ 605 8923 ⓒ 09.00–18.00 ⓦ www.hertz.ee

---

◗ *Raekoja plats – Town Hall Square – is at the heart of the city*

THE CITY OF
Tallinn

The Old Town

Tallinn has had a turbulent past. Much of the time the city has either been under siege or lived with the threat of invasion. To cope, the residents built massive walls to surround the town. With some 46 towers, medieval Tallinn was possibly the most fortified town in all of Northern Europe. Today, only 20 towers and nearly 2 km (1¼ miles) of the walls remain. A few of the towers, such as Fat Margaret (see page 76), serve as museums, while many others have been transformed into restaurants, hotels, homes and offices. The oldest of the towers, Nunne, Sauna and Kuldjala, remain open to the public.

The Old Town may appear compact on the map, but you can spend hours, if not days, exploring its intriguing nooks and crannies. Your adventure on foot will give you a glimpse of life in Tallinn. From up-and-coming entrepreneurs who can afford to renovate ancient buildings, to the ageing ladies who come to beg outside the Lutheran cathedral, the Old Town is a mix of the Tallinn of yesterday and today.

The joy of sightseeing in the Old Town area of Tallinn is that it is comfortably walkable. The narrow, twisted, and sometimes quite vertically inclined streets allow for minimal car traffic, and no public transport.

SIGHTS & ATTRACTIONS

Aleksander Nevski Katedraal (Alexander Nevsky Cathedral)

Built in 1900, this relative newcomer does not quite fit architecturally into the rest of the medieval Old Town. A typical onion-domed Russian Orthodox Church, it sits next to Toompea Castle and can be seen from most parts of the city. Inside is an impressive

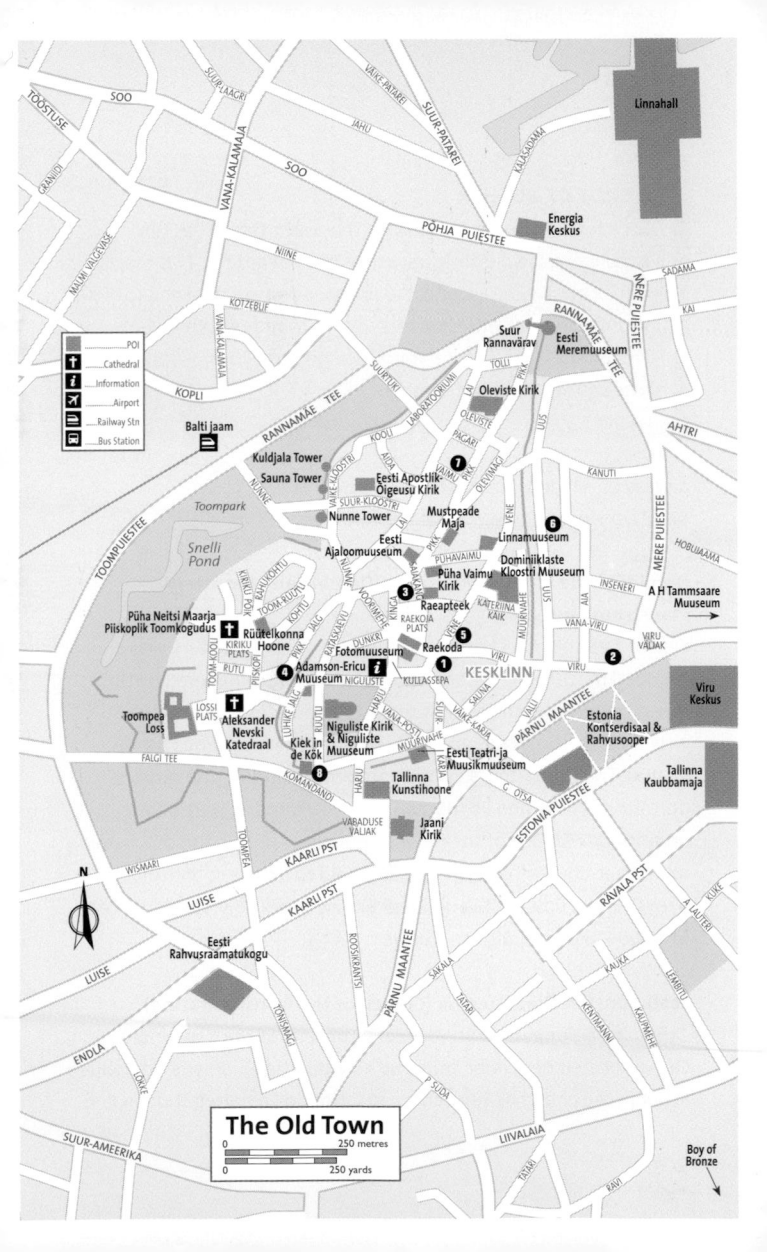

The Old Town

| 0 | 250 metres |
| 0 | 250 yards |

A SPOT OF BOTHER

Look for two long cobblestones that form the letter 'L' in a corner of Town Hall Square near the Raeapteek. This marks the location where a priest was beheaded, on the spot, for having killed a waitress who brought food not to his liking. The moral: don't enter the priesthood until you've worked through your anger issues.

display of religious icons. ⓐ Lossi plats 10 ⓣ 644 3484
ⓛ 08.00–19.00 ⓦ www.hot.ee/nsobor

Dominiiklaste Kloostri Muuseum (Dominican Monastery Claustrum Museum)

One of Tallinn's oldest existing buildings, this monastery was founded in 1246. The part of the monastery administered by the museum includes the courtyard and surrounding passageways, where fascinating 15th- and 16th-century stone carvings are on display. The monastery's inner chambers, including the monk's dormitory, priory and library, can only be visited as part of an organised tour. One of the most interesting spots is the downstairs room that houses the 'energy pillar', said to be the source of a mysterious power. ⓐ Vene 16/18 ⓣ 644 4606 ⓦ www.kloostri.ee
ⓛ 10.00–18.00. Admission charge

Eesti Apostlik-Õigeusu Kirik (Church of the Transfiguration)

Originally belonging to St Michael's Convent of the Cistercian Order (located next door and now housing the Gustavus Adolphus School), the church was given to an Orthodox congregation in 1716.

◆ *The cathedral illustrates Russian influence on the country*

The church has retained its original form, aside from the addition of a baroque spire in 1776 and exterior renovations in the early 1800s. The carved-wood iconostasis is one of the most impressive of its kind. The church is only open on Sunday mornings for a service, but this is a particularly lovely time to experience the interior in all its glory. ⓐ Suur-Kloostri 14-1 ⓣ 646 4003 ⓦ www.eaok.ee ⓛ 09.00–13.00 Sun

Kiek in de Kök (Peep into the Kitchen)

This restored tower provides an excellent introduction to the history of Tallinn's elaborate defence system of walls and towers. The unusual name comes from the vantage point it offers if you climb to the top of its stairs. It houses a contemporary art museum which is currently undergoing renovation work and is due to re-open sometime in 2010 – call in advance or ask at the tourist office to check whether or not it is open. Meanwhile, guided tours of the passages inside the bastions are available. For an English-language tour, make sure you call to organise this in advance. ⓐ Komandandi 2 ⓣ 644 6686 ⓦ www.linnamuuseum.ee/kok ⓛ Tours: 11.00–16.00 Tues–Sun

Mustpeade Maja (House of the Blackheads)

The Brotherhood of the Blackheads was a merchants' guild founded in 1343, and the house was built as lodgings for visiting merchants. Over the centuries it evolved into a social drinking club, finally dissolving in 1940 when the Russians moved in. The house is elaborately decorated in Renaissance style, both inside and out. It's not normally open to the public, but you can see the interior

ⓞ *House of the Blackheads*

if you attend one of the regular chamber concerts (see page 80).
🄰 Pikk 26 🕻 631 3199 🅦 www.mustpeademaja.ee

Niguliste Kirik (St Nicholas's Church)

Started in the 13th century and rebuilt in the 15th century, this imposing church is now a museum housing Tallinn's collection of medieval art. There are several carved and painted altars, friezes, tomb-top effigies, and other interesting works. The present classical building dates from the 1820s, but a Russian Orthodox church stood here in the early 1400s. The young church houses many objects of artistic value predating it, including 16th-century icons. 🄰 Niguliste 3 🕻 631 4330 🅦 www.ekm.ee/niguliste
🕒 10.00–17.00 Wed–Sun; services: 09.30, 18.00 Sat, 10.00 Sun. Admission charge for visits

Oleviste Kirik (St Olaf's Church)

The spire of this church is Tallinn's landmark and at one time it may have been the tallest spire in the whole of Europe. Although the church dates from 1267, the interior is from the 1840s. 🄰 Lai 50
🕻 641 2241 🅦 www.oleviste.ee 🕒 Church: 10.00–14.00 Tues–Fri; tower: 10.00–18.00. Admission charge for tower

Püha Vaimu Kirik (Church of the Holy Ghost)

Built in the 1360s, this historic church is the only one in Tallinn with an original exterior. The clock, set into the wall in 1680, is the oldest timepiece in Estonia. Although simple and humble on the outside, the interior is richly decorated and contains precious works of medieval art. 🄰 Pühavaimu 2 🕻 646 4430 🕒 09.00–15.00 Mon–Fri, summer; 10.00–14.00 Mon–Fri, winter

Raeapteek (Town Hall Pharmacy)

One of the oldest continuously running pharmacies in Europe
is on Town Hall Square. Records exist showing it dates back
to at least 1422, but it may have opened even earlier than that.
In medieval times the ailing could buy burnt bees and bat powder
for treatments, and if you didn't have a specific illness you could
buy a glass of spiced claret. The pharmacy offers modern
medications these days, and part of the store is a museum.
ⓐ Raekoja plats 11 ⓣ 631 4860 ⓛ 09.00–17.00 Tues–Sat

Raekoda & Raekoja plats (Town Hall & Town Hall Square)

Town Hall Square is as old as Tallinn itself. Surrounded by medieval
buildings painted in pastel colours, the square is an Estonian
landmark, and a popular rallying point for Estonian patriotism.

BOY OF BRONZE

Originally erected in 1947, this monument of a Red Army
soldier used to stand in front of the National Library. It has
always inspired controversy: to some, it represented the
liberation of Estonia from the Nazis by Soviet forces; to others,
it came to symbolise Soviet repression. In April 2007, the
Estonian government decided to move the statue to a new
location at the military cemetery. Young people, mostly
Russian-speakers, flocked to the site and rioted for two nights
in protest. Eventually, after a handbags-at-dawn propaganda
battle with Russia, things settled down and the Russian-
speaking population is now getting used to the statue's
new location. ⓐ Filtri tee 14 ⓦ Bus: 13

On the south side stands the Town Hall, built in the 15th century. Look up to see the Gothic arches, steeple and weather vane. Note the water-spouting green painted dragons just below the roof line. In summer you can visit an exhibition in the cellar, the ceremonial halls, and a tower offering great views over the Old Town.

ⓐ Raekoja plats 1 ❶ 645 7900 Ⓦ www.tallinn.ee/raekoda
🕐 Town hall: 10.00–16.00 Mon–Sat, summer; tower: 11.00–18.00 summer. Admission charge

Suur Rannavärav (Great Sea Gate)

At the northern end of the Old Town, the Great Sea Gate is a 16th-century arch flanked by two towers. The larger of the two towers is Fat Margaret, a barrel-shaped tower whose walls are 4 m (13 ft) thick. When it was no longer needed for defensive purposes, it became the city's jail. Today, it houses the Estonian Maritime Museum (see page 79). ⓐ Pikk 70

Toompea Loss (Toompea Castle)

Sitting at the very top of Toompea, the hill that overlooks the city, this castle has guarded Tallinn for most of its history. It was an Estonian stockade until it was captured in 1219 by the Danes, who built the first stone castle. Over the centuries, the castle has been rebuilt and renovated many times; the latest refurbishment was by Russia's Catherine the Great, who gave it its pink baroque façade. It is dominated by three defensive towers, the tallest of which, Tall Herman, dates from 1371. ⓐ Lossi plats ❶ 631 6537 ❶ Admission only with guided tour; call for tour times

---

▶ *It is easy to spot which of the towers is Fat Margaret*

Toompea Castle looms tall over Tallinn

CULTURE

For information on cultural events and exhibitions or to book tickets, see ⓦ www.concert.ee or ⓦ www.piletilevi.ee

Adamson-Ericu Muuseum (Adamson-Eric Museum)
The permanent collection of works by world-famous artist Adamson-Eric is housed in a 16th-century building within the Old Town. ⓐ Lühike jalg 3 ⓣ 644 5838 ⓦ www.ekm.ee/adamson-eric ⓛ 11.00–18.00 Wed–Sun. Admission charge

Eesti Ajaloomuuseum (Estonian History Museum)
Situated in the House of the Great Guild, the museum's exhibitions cover Estonia's earliest history up to the 18th century, with explanations translated into English. The building itself was a gathering place for Tallinn's wealthy merchants. ⓐ Pikk 17 ⓣ 641 1630 ⓦ www.eam.ee ⓛ 11.00–18.00 summer; 11.00–18.00 Thur–Tues, winter. Admission charge

Eesti Meremuuseum (Estonian Maritime Museum)
Tallinn's significant seafaring history is put on display in this museum housed over four floors of the 16th-century Fat Margaret tower. Don't miss the antique diving equipment or the spectacular views from the roof. ⓐ Pikk 70 ⓣ 641 1408 ⓦ www.meremuuseum.ee ⓛ 10.00–18.00 Wed–Sun. Admission charge

Estonia Kontserdisaal (Estonia Concert Hall)
The number one place to hear classical music and operatic performances. In summer, book tickets in advance. ⓐ Estonia pst. 4 ⓣ 614 7760 ⓦ www.concert.ee

Fotomuuseum (Museum of Photography)

Nowadays, the former city prison, which dates from the 14th century, houses a compact exhibition on Estonian photography. The first camera arrived in Tallinn just one year after debuting in France and the art developed quickly here. Don't miss the contemporary exhibitions and shop. ⓐ City Prison, Raekoja tn. 4/6 ⓣ 644 8767 ⓦ www.linnamuuseum.ee ⓛ 10.30–18.00 Thur–Tues. Admission charge

Linnamuuseum (Tallinn City Museum)

Housed in a 14th-century merchant's house, this museum manages to compact centuries of the city's history into a complete and lively array of exhibits. Most of the exhibits have English captions. ⓐ Vene 17 ⓣ 644 6553 ⓦ www.linnamuuseum.ee ⓛ 10.30–18.00 Wed–Mon

Mustpeade Maja (House of the Blackheads)

This gloriously ornate guildhall (see page 73) stages classical music concerts nearly every night. It also hosts monthly social dances, so be sure to get a copy of the events calendar. ⓐ Pikk 26 ⓣ 631 3199 ⓦ www.mustpeademaja.ee

Niguliste Muuseum (St Nicholas's Museum)

This 13th-century Gothic church, which houses a fascinating collection of medieval art, holds regular organ concerts every Saturday and Sunday at 16.00. ⓐ Niguliste 3 ⓣ 631 4340 ⓦ www.ekm.ee/niguliste ⓛ 10.00–17.00 Wed–Sun

Rahvusooper Estonia (Estonian National Opera)

This company has its home at the Estonia Concert Hall. ⓐ Estonia pst. 4 ⓣ 683 1201 ⓦ www.opera.ee

Rüütelkonna Hoone

This grand building perched on Toompea Hill serves as the main branch of the Art Museum of Estonia. The collection provides an excellent overview of Estonian art. ⓐ Kiriku plats 1 ⓣ 644 9340 ⓛ 11.00–18.00 Wed–Sun. Admission charge

RETAIL THERAPY

In retail terms, Tallinn doesn't just offer itself on a plate. You have to look a little to find the city's shopping possibilities, but of course there's a thrill in that chase.

If you are looking for a special souvenir, the streets of the Old Town are the place to go. Linen, wool clothing and amber jewellery are local specialities, and you will find these at many shops, especially along Pikk and Dunkri. The best place for knitted gems is the open-air woollen market on Müürivahe just north of Viru Gate.

Antiik This charming outlet offers a wide range of old – and even antique – objects that make really classy gifts and souvenirs. ⓐ Kinga 5 ⓣ 646 6232 ⓦ www.antiqueshop.ee ⓛ 10.00–18.00

Apollo Bookstore Lots of novels and guidebooks in English. ⓐ Viru 23 ⓦ www.apollo.ee ⓛ 10.00–20.00 Mon–Fri, 10.00–19.00 Sat, 11.00–17.00 Sun

Draakoni Gallery This quaint gallery also houses a shop where you can buy works of art. ⓐ Pikk 18 ⓣ 646 4110 ⓦ www.eaa.ee ⓛ 10.00–18.00 Mon–Fri, 10.00–17.00 Sat

Kalev Chocolate Factory Museum Indulge in a wide variety of

Estonian chocolate; you can also see marzipan being painted here.
ⓐ Pikk 16 **ⓘ** 646 4192 **ⓒ** 10.00–17.00

Katariina Guild A collection of several craft workshops along Catherine's passage, selling ceramics, leatherwork, stained glass and jewellery. **ⓐ** Katariina käik, Vene 12 **ⓘ** 644 5365 **ⓒ** 11.00–18.00 summer; 12.00–18.00 Mon–Sat, winter

● *Flowers aren't just saved for special occasions*

Lino Great selection of knits and linens. ⓐ Pikk 12 ⓣ 646 2012
ⓛ 09.00–19.00

Madeli Käsitöö This is a fabulous place to go if you're looking for
authentically regional souvenirs of your stay. No tat. ⓐ Voorimehe 4
ⓣ 646 4543 ⓛ 10.00–18.00

Sepa Äri Products of Estonia's long tradition of smithing.
ⓐ Olevimägi 11 ⓣ 680 0971 ⓛ 10.00–20.00 Mon–Fri, 10.00–17.00
Sat, 10.00–15.00 Sun

Veta Probably the best linens in town. The tablecloths and clothes,
in particular, are excellent. ⓐ Pikk 4 ⓣ 646 4140 ⓦ www.veta.ee
ⓛ 10.00–19.00

Zizi Ethnographic textiles for the home. ⓐ Vene 12 ⓣ 644 1222
ⓛ 10.00–18.00 Mon–Sat, 10.00–16.00 Sun

TAKING A BREAK

Elsebet £ ❶ Eat in, or take away some of the best pastries in
Tallinn. Since your bag of goodies probably won't make it back
to the hotel, take a seat at one of the candle-lit wooden tables.
ⓐ Viru 2/Vanaturu 6 ⓣ 646 6800 ⓦ www.peppersack.ee
ⓛ 08.00–18.00 Mon–Sat, 10.00–18.00 Sun

Hesburger £ ❷ Run by a Finnish team, offering burgers and other
snacks. ⓐ Viru 27A ⓣ 627 2516 ⓦ www.hesburger.ee ⓛ 09.00–23.00
Sun–Thur, 09.00–01.00 Fri & Sat

Kehrwieder £ ❸ Wonderful pastries right on Town Hall Square, plus its own sandwich shop right across the ancient passage. Among the friendliest service in town. ⓐ Saiakang 1 ⓦ www.kehrwieder.ee ⓛ 08.00–23.00 Sun–Thur, 08.00–01.00 Fri & Sat

Bogapott ££ ❹ Hidden away in a part of the medieval town wall on Toompea is this café selling pastries and sandwiches. It doubles as an art shop with a ceramics studio. ⓐ Pikk jalg 9 ⓣ 631 3181 ⓦ www.bogapott.ee ⓛ 10.00–22.00 Mon–Sat, 10.00–17.00 Sun

Chocolaterie Café Pierre ££ ❺ Quaint, pretty and in need of a lot more chairs. A master *chocolatier* makes truffles from scratch. Just the sugar hit you'll need to carry on sightseeing. ⓐ Vene 6 (in the courtyard) ⓣ 641 8061 ⓛ 08.00–23.00

Kohvicum ££ ❻ Located just below Tallinn's Music House, this café offers musical performances in the courtyard in summer. ⓐ Uus 16C ⓣ 642 7026 ⓦ www.kohvik.ee ⓛ 10.00–23.00

Le Bonaparte £££ ❼ This is an ideal café to grab a coffee and pastry in the middle of the day. ⓐ Pikk 45 ⓣ 646 4444 ⓦ www.bonaparte.ee ⓛ 08.00–22.00 Mon–Fri, 10.00–22.00 Sat, 10.00–18.00 Sun

AFTER DARK

RESTAURANTS

Grillhaus Daube ££ ❽ A roomy grill house with warm décor and an even warmer fireplace. Be prepared for hearty steaks and huge plates of ribs and other meaty dishes. ⓐ Rüütli 11 ⓣ 645 5531 ⓦ www.daube.ee ⓛ 12.00–23.00

BARS & CLUBS

Club 360 A place to dance all night long to music spun by some of the best local and international DJs around. ⓐ Müürivahe 22 ⓣ 631 3360 ⓦ www.club360.ee ⓛ 22.00–05.00 Fri & Sat

Kompressor Students love the simple décor, oversized tables and cheap drinks here. Add to that the good and incredibly cheap pancakes, and you've got the makings of a budget night out. ⓐ Rataskaevu 3 ⓣ 646 4210 ⓛ 11.00–00.00

St Patrick's Irish of vibe, Estonian of customer base. The food is good and every fourth Saku Originaal is free. ⓐ Suur-Karja 8 ⓣ 641 8173 ⓦ www.patricks.ee ⓛ 11.00–02.00 Sun–Thur, 11.00–04.00 Fri & Sat

Valli Baar At first glance this Old Town pub doesn't look worthy of a second glance. But at night, when students drop in for cheap drinks and elderly regulars start to swing to the live accordion music, the atmosphere moves into the realm of the surreal. ⓐ Müürivahe 16 ⓣ 641 8379 ⓛ 11.00–23.00

Von Krahli Baar If you don't dig alternative bands in a studenty atmosphere, then at least stop by for the cheap, good food during the day. ⓐ Rataskaevu 10/12 ⓣ 626 9090 ⓦ www.vonkrahl.ee ⓛ 12.00–01.00 Sun–Thur, 12.00–03.00 Fri & Sat

City Centre

There is more to Tallinn than its Old Town. Step outside that compact area to discover a modern city humming with activity, where Radisson or TGI Friday's signs are to be found alongside beautiful old buildings such as the pseudo-Gothic **Jaani Kirik** (St John's Church ⓐ Vabaduse väljak 1 ❶ 644 6206 Ⓦ www.tallinnajaani.ee ❶ 10.00–14.00 Tues, Thur & Fri, 10.00–17.00 Wed; services: 10.00 Sun). Public transport options are slightly better here than in the Old Town, but in most cases it's still easier and quicker to walk to your destination.

CULTURE

Linnahall

This great grey monolith at the edge of the harbour plays host to pop concerts and big-name artists. ⓐ Mere pst. 20 ❶ 641 2250 Ⓦ www.linnahall.ee Ⓝ Tram: 1, 2; bus: 3

Saku Suurhall

This concert and sports arena is best known for having hosted the Eurovision Song Contest in 2002. The venue holds cultural events and has its own sports bar and restaurant. ⓐ Paldiski mnt. 104B ❶ 660 0200 Ⓦ www.sakusuurhall.ee Ⓝ Trolleybus: 6, 7; bus: 21, 22

Tallinna Kunstihoone (Tallinn Art Hall Foundation)

This imposing 1930s building houses avant-garde and daring exhibitions from Estonia and abroad. ⓐ Vabaduse väljak 6 ❶ 644 2818 ❶ 12.00–18.00 Wed–Sun Ⓝ Trolleybus: 1, 2, 3, 6; tram: 3, 4

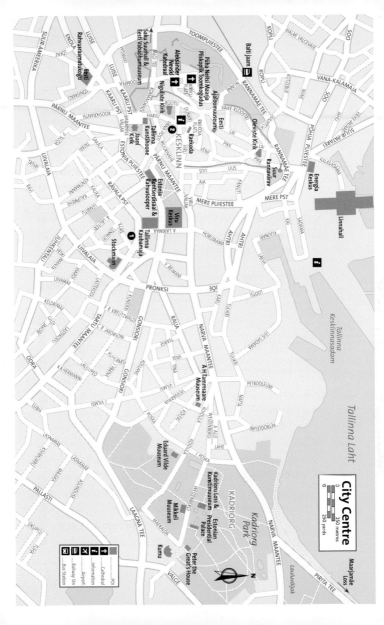

A H TAMMSAARE – ESTONIA'S KAFKA

Anton Hansen Tammsaare (1878–1940) is generally considered to be the greatest Estonian writer of the 20th century. His work is set against a background of – and is infused by – his own experience of almost life-long physical and psychological suffering. His books are exquisitely poignant, and the most famous of them make up the five-part epic *Truth and Justice*. The A H Tammsaare Muuseum chronicles his life and work and includes the apartment where he spent his last eight years, painstakingly restored to its 1930s original décor. ⓐ Koidula 12a ⓣ 601 3232 ⓦ www.linnamuuseum.ee/tammsaare ⓛ 11.00–17.00 Wed–Mon ⓝ Tram: 1, 3. Admission charge

RETAIL THERAPY

Tallinn has three large department stores within walking distance of its Old Town: **Stockmann** (ⓐ Liivalaia 53 ⓣ 633 9539 ⓦ www.stockmann.ee ⓛ 09.00–20.00 Mon–Sat, 10.00–20.00 Sun ⓝ Tram: 2, 4); **Tallinna Kaubamaja** (ⓐ Gonsiori 2 ⓣ 667 3100 ⓦ www.kaubamaja.ee ⓛ 09.00–21.00 ⓝ Tram: 1, 2, 3, 4); and **Viru Keskus** (ⓐ Viru väljak 4 ⓣ 610 1444 ⓦ www.virukeskus.com ⓛ 08.00–21.00 ⓝ Tram: 1, 2, 3, 4).

Lasering Estonian and international rock and pop CDs and DVDs – everything from indie to film soundtracks. ⓐ Pärnu mnt. 38 ⓣ 627 9279 ⓛ 10.00–19.00 Mon–Fri, 10.00–17.00 Sat ⓝ Tram: 1, 2

◆ *Contrasting building styles in the city centre*

Rahva Raamat The city's best and biggest bookstore is found on the top floor of the Viru Keskus shopping mall. It has a large selection of foreign-language books, as well as two popular cafés. ⓐ Viru väljak 4 ⓣ 610 1444 ⓛ 09.00–21.00 ⓝ Tram: 1, 2, 3, 4

AFTER DARK

RESTAURANTS

Lounge 24 £££ ❶ Named after its location on the 24th floor of the Radisson Blu hotel, this is the place to come for a view. The menu is limited, the service is generally good, and the vista always without rival. ⓐ Rävala pst. 3 ⓣ 682 3424 ⓦ www.madissoni.ee ⓛ 12.00–02.00 ⓝ Trolleybus: 1, 3, 6

Stereo Lounge £££ ❷ Everything here is white – walls, ceilings, tables and chairs. Fortunately the guests are colourful, the cocktails are great, and the kitchen dishes up anything from British-style breakfasts to innovative sushi omelettes. ⓐ Harju 6 ⓣ 631 0549 ⓦ www.stereolounge.ee ⓛ 10.00–02.00 Mon–Thur, 11.00–03.00 Fri & Sat, 11.00–02.00 Sun ⓝ Trolleybus: 1, 2, 3, 6; tram: 3, 4

PUBS & BARS

The Englishman Pub Serving English beer and playing English music, this is not bad at all for a hotel pub. The décor is a cross between a cricket museum and a gentlemen's club, with English newspapers and magazines available, but that doesn't stop the nightlife becoming downright raucous. ⓐ Reval Hotel Olümpia, Liivalaia 33 ⓣ 631 5833 ⓦ www.revalhotels.com ⓛ 18.00–01.00 Mon–Thur, 18.00–03.00 Fri & Sat ⓝ Tram: 2, 4

Novell Though situated by Tallinn's busiest road, this lounge bar and restaurant has a leisurely atmosphere and relaxing background music. Delicious snacks and meals are served with a smile. ⓐ Narva mnt. 7c ① 633 9891 ⓦ www.novell.ee ⓛ 12.00–23.00 Mon–Thur, 12.00–01.00 Fri & Sat ⓝ Tram: 1, 2, 3, 4

Rock Café In a giant stone-walled paper factory, this club run by a radio DJ is the country's hottest destination for live music. ⓐ Tartu mnt. 80D, 3rd floor ⓦ www.rockcafe.ee ⓛ 21.00–04.00 Thur, 22.00–04.00 Fri–Sun

Vertigo Nine floors above the ground and with a huge terrace, this is a superb place to come for sunset drinks followed by – if you can afford it – a gourmet meal of up to nine courses, supplemented by an ambitious wine list. ⓐ Rävala pst 4 ① 666 3456 ⓦ www.vertigo.ee ⓛ 12.00–23.00 Mon–Thur, 12.00–00.00 Fri & Sat, 11.00–20.00 Sun ⓝ Trolleybus: 1, 3, 6

◗ *The sports bar at Saku Suurhall (see page 86)*

Suburbs East & West

KADRIORG

Kadriorg is a large public park about 1 km (½ mile) east of the Old Town. Created by Tsar Peter the Great in the early 18th century, the heavily forested park is criss-crossed with paths, and dotted with statues, ponds and fountains. In the centre is the magnificent Kadriorg Palace. The park contains other historic and important buildings, such as Peter the Great's House, the Estonian Presidential Palace, and several other museums.

SIGHTS & ATTRACTIONS
Kadrioru Park (Kadriorg Park)
Only a small part of the large Kadriorg Park was designed as a formal park in its time – most of it was intended to preserve the look of the natural landscape. Lining the promenade leading from the popular Swan Lake to the palace (Weizenbergi Street) are many of the palace's auxiliary buildings. The restoration workshop of the Estonian Art Museum is located in the palace's guest house and the park pavilion next door. Opposite the palace gates is a small guard house, the palace's kitchen building and ice cellar. Ⓝ Tram: 1, 3

CULTURE
Kadrioru Loss & Kunstimuuseum (Kadriorg Palace & Art Museum)
Peter I began building the palace in 1718, named Ekaterinenthal, or Catherinenthal, in honour of Catherine I. Currently, the baroque Kadriorg Palace houses the Kadriorg Art Museum, the foreign art collection of the Estonian Art Museum. The collection contains more than 900 Western European and Russian paintings from the

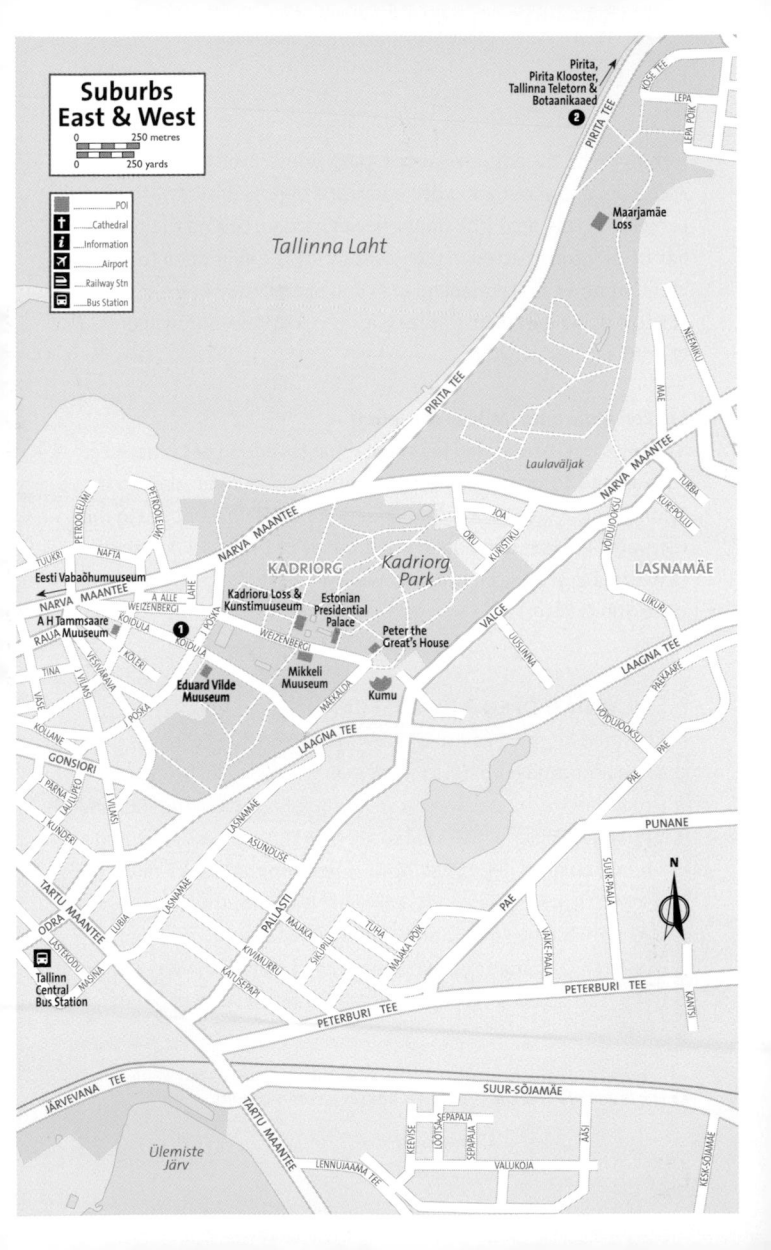

Suburbs
East & West

0 | 250 metres
0 | 250 yards

POI
Cathedral
Information
Airport
Railway Stn
Bus Station

Tallinna Laht

Pirita,
Pirita Klooster,
Tallinna Teletorn &
Botaanikaaed
❷

LEPA

KOSE TEE

LEPA PÕIK

Maarjamäe
Loss

PIRITA TEE

NEEMKU

PIRITA TEE

MÄE

Laulaväljak

NARVA MAANTEE

VÕIDUJOOKSU

KUREPÕLU

TURBA

PETROOLEUMI

TUUKRI

NAFTA

Eesti Vabaõhumuuseum
←

NARVA MAANTEE

A H Tammsaare
RAUA Muuseum

TINA

VASE

VÄSE

KÕLANE

Ä ALLE

WEIZENBERGI

LAHE

KOIDULA

KOLERI

KOIDULA

POSKA

J VILMSI

VESIVÄRAVA

KADRIORG

POSKA

❶

Kadrioru Loss &
Kunstimuuseum

Estonian
Presidential
Palace

Mikkeli
Muuseum

MALEVA

*Kadriorg
Park*

Peter the
Great's House

Kumu

OKSA

KUNSTKU

ORU

JOA

VALGE

LUSIINNA

LASNAMÄE

LIKURI

LAAGNA TEE

PAEKAAR

VÕIDUJOOKSU

PAE

Eduard Vilde
Muuseum

GONSIORI

PÄRNU MNT

LUBJA

PALDI

KUNDERI

J VILMSI

LASNAMÄE

LASNAMÄE

ASUNDUSE

PALLASTI

MAJAKA

KIVIMURRU

KATUSEPAPI

TUHA

SIKUPILLI

MAJAKA PÕIK

LAAGNA TEE

PAE

PUNANE

SUUR-PAALA

VÄLKE-PAALA

PETERBURI TEE

KANTSI

N

TARTU MAANTEE

ODRA MAANTEE

KÄSTIKODU

MAGASINI

🚌
Tallinn
Central
Bus Station

PETERBURI TEE

JÄRVEVANA TEE

TARTU MAANTEE

*Ülemiste
Järv*

LENNUJAAMA TEE

SUUR-SÕJAMÄE

KEEVISE

LÕÕTSA

SEPAPAJA

SEPAPAJA

VALUKOJA

AIA

KESK-SÕJAMÄE

16th to the 20th centuries, about 3,500 prints, over 3,000 sculptures and gems, and about 1,600 decorative arts objects (historical furniture, porcelain, glass, etc.). The upper flower garden, behind the palace, has been reconstructed in 18th-century style, and is open to visitors in the summer. ❸ Weizenbergi 37 ❶ 606 6400 ❿ www.ekm.ee
🕔 10.00–17.00 Tues–Sun, summer, 10.00–17.00 Wed–Sun, winter
Ⓝ Tram: 1, 3

Mikkeli Muuseum (Mikkel Museum)

Johannes Mikkel donated his substantial collection of Chinese, Russian and European paintings, prints, icons and porcelain to the Estonian Art Museum in 1994. The collection is now housed in the renovated kitchen building in the grounds of the Kadriorg Palace.
❸ Weizenbergi 28 ❶ 601 5844 ❿ ww.ekm.ee 🕔 10.00–17.00
Wed–Sun Ⓝ Tram: 1, 3

ESTONIAN OPEN-AIR MUSEUM

Located on the western outskirts of Tallinn, the Eesti Vabaõhumuuseum (Estonian Open-air Museum) brings together over 100 Estonian village buildings from the 18th and 19th centuries. Exhibits illustrate how the villagers lived, and how buildings developed from simple longhouses to more sophisticated farmsteads. There are also watermills and windmills. The Kolu Café serves traditional bean soup and beer. ❸ Vabaõhumuuseumi tee 12 ❶ 654 9100 ❿ www.evm.ee
🕔 10.00–20.00 Ⓝ Trolleybus: 6, 7; bus: 21, 21B. Admission charge

🛈 *The home of Peter the Great now houses an art museum*

TAKING A BREAK & AFTER DARK
Lydia £££ ❶ Next to Kadriorg Park, this restaurant has live music at the weekend to accompany the fine Estonian dining it offers. ⓐ Koidula 13a ⓣ 626 8990 ⓦ www.lydia.ee ⓛ 12.00–20.00 Mon, 12.00–22.00 Tues–Thur & Sat, 12.00–23.00 Fri, 12.00–19.00 Sun

PIRITA

This seaside suburb is located 6 km (3½ miles) from Tallinn's city centre. In the early 20th century, Pirita began to develop into a destination for Sunday rides and swimming. Today, it's a great place to spend free time, with its bathing beaches, coastline, pine-forested parks and picturesque Pirita River valley. Tallinn's Botanic Gardens straddle the Pirita River. To get to Pirita, take bus 34A or 38 from the main bus stop outside Viru Keskus (see page 88).

SIGHTS & ATTRACTIONS
Botaanikaaed (Botanic Gardens)
Located in Pirita, near the TV Tower, the gardens feature virtually every type of tree and plant found in Estonia. The grounds are immaculately kept, and in the centre is a Palm House (where they hold changing exhibitions), a rose garden and an alpine garden. ⓐ Kloostrimetsa tee 52 ⓣ 606 2679 ⓛ Glasshouses: 11.00–18.00; gardens: 11.00–18.00 winter; 11.00–19.00 summer ⓝ Bus: 34A, 38

Lauluväljak (Song Festival Grounds)
This is where the 'Singing Revolution' (see page 21) began in 1988. The Lauluväljak is comprised of both a huge outdoor arena and

a modern indoor concert hall. ⓐ Narva mnt. 95 ❶ 611 2102
ⓦ www.lauluvaljak.ee ⓝ Bus: 1A, 5, 8, 19, 34A, 35, 38, 44, 51, 60, 63

Pirita Klooster (Pirita Convent)

Established in 1407, the church was destroyed in the late 1500s,
and only the western limestone gable and side walls remain. In the
17th century, a farmers' cemetery developed in front of the ruins.
Apparently, secret underground passageways lead from the convent
to the city. ⓐ Merivälja tee 18 ❶ 605 5044 ⓦ www.piritaklooster.ee
🕐 09.00–19.00 summer; 12.00–16.00 winter ⓝ Bus: 1, 8, 34A, 38.
Admission charge

🔺 St Bridget's Convent is possibly linked to Tallinn by secret passages

● Dusk in Pirita's harbour

Tallinna Teletorn (Tallinn TV Tower)

The 314 m (1,030 ft) TV Tower was built for the 1980 Olympic Games. It is closed to the public for the foreseeable future, but is still an impressive sight from the outside. ⓐ Kloostrimetsa 58a ❶ 600 5511, ⓦ www.teletorn.ee ⓝ Bus: 34A, 38

TAKING A BREAK & AFTER DARK

Kalevi Yacht Club ££ ❷ It has become more expensive over the years, but this yacht club is an ideal place to escape the pace of city cafés. Located on the seaside near the Pirita River bridge, it's great for a bite after touring the Pirita neighbourhood. ⓐ Pirita tee 17 ❶ 623 9158 ⓦ www.jahtklubibaar.ee ❶ 11.00–23.00 ⓝ Bus: 34A, 38

❶ Seventy per cent of Estonia is coastline, so quick escapes are easy

OUT OF TOWN
trips

Pärnu

Pärnu is Estonia's best-known summer resort. The attraction lies in its unpolluted shallow sea bay, which is warm by June, and in its fine, white sandy beaches. Sunbathers started coming here in the 19th century, and they continue to flock here every summer.

Aside from the nightclubs and other party scenes, Pärnu offers museums, theatres and live concerts. Spas and recuperation centres are also important here.

GETTING THERE

Pärnu is accessible by car from central Tallinn – take Pärnu maantee (Highway 4) south for 130 km (80 miles). Regular bus services operate between Tallinn and Pärnu, and the journey takes under two hours.

Located right in the centre, the Tourist Information Centre provides tips and brochures and has a booth at the beach in summer.

Tourist Information Centre ⓐ Rüütli 16 ⓣ 447 3000 ⓦ www.parnu.ee

SIGHTS & ATTRACTIONS

Mini Zoo

This is home to some fabulous snakes, spiders and crocodiles.
ⓐ Akadeemia 1 ⓣ 551 6033 ⓦ www.hot.ee/minizoo ⓛ 10.00–19.00 summer; 12.00–16.00 Mon–Fri, 11.00–16.00 Sat & Sun, winter. Admission charge

Parks

A large part of what makes Pärnu such a relaxing place to visit are its vast, green areas designed for strolling. The most notable of these

The River Pärnu runs through the city

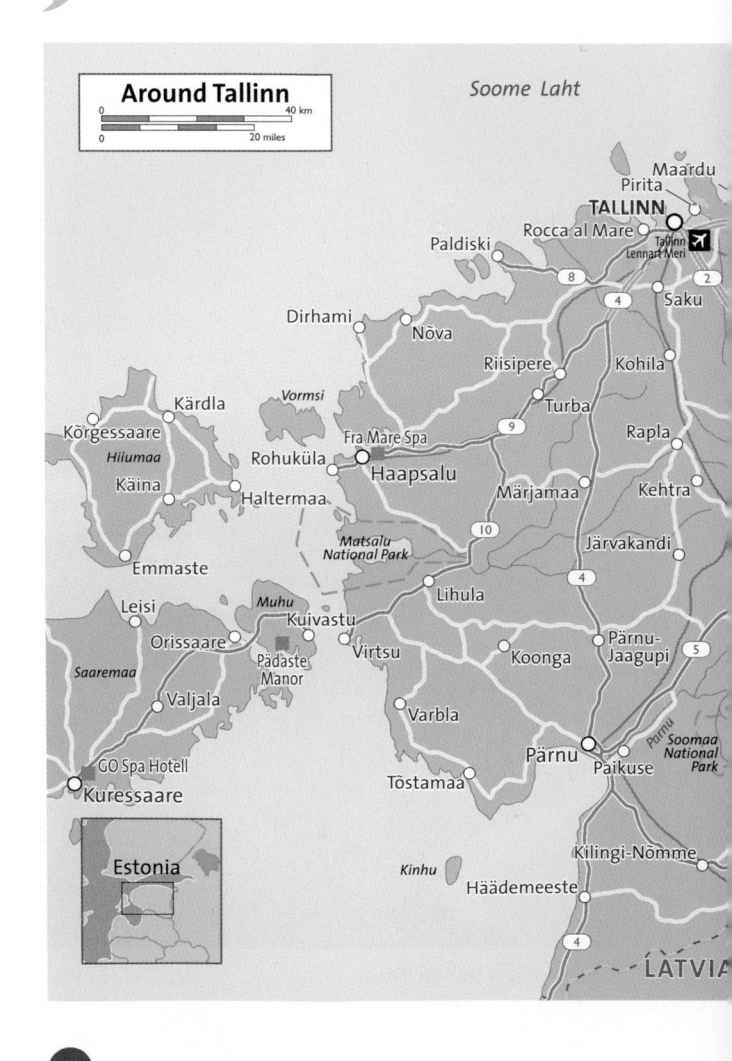

Löksa
Võsu
Luhemaa National Park
Palmse
Estonian Golf & Country Club
Viitna
Kunda
Kalvi Manor
Saka Cliff Hotel & Spa
Kohtla-Järve
Toila Sanatorium
Kehra
LÄÄNE-VIRUMAA
Kiviõli
Sillamäe
Rakvere
Jõhvi
Tapa
Ahtme
Aravete
Tamsalu
Tudu
Iisaku
Roosna-Alliku
Väike-Maarja
Vasknarva
Rakke
Avinurme
Kauksi
Paide
ESTONIA
Mustvee
Türi
Peipsi Järv
RUSSIA
Gdov
Jõgeva
Kallaste
Põltsamaa
Suure-Jaani
Koosa
Emajõgi
Tartu
Viljandi
Puhja
Vörtsjärv
Ülenurme
Haaslava
Võnnu
Lange
Mustla
Rannu
Tartu Lennundusmuuseum
Räpina
Otepää
Põlva

○ City
○ Large Town
○ Small Town
■ POI
Motorway
Main Road
Minor Road
✈ Airport
Railway

is Koidula Park, adjacent to the downtown area, with its colourful flowerbeds and fountain. Another, Rannapark, is no longer a park as such, but now boasts **Nurmenuku puhkekeskus** (☏ 507 7851 ⓦ www.nurmenukupk.ee ⏰ 11.00–19.00), a pony ranch for children.

Rüütli tänav (Knight Street)

Historic downtown Pärnu is defined by its main pedestrian thoroughfare, Rüütli tänav (Knight Street). The 400 m (440 yds) stretch of the street between Ringi and Vee, and a few streets that branch off from here, are home to a hodge-podge of intriguing buildings dating from the 17th to the 20th centuries. This is also where you'll find Pärnu's most exclusive shops.

CULTURE

Agape Keskus (Agape Centre)
The church has an active congregation and a lively cultural centre, with frequent performances in summer. ⓐ Männi 2 ☏ 445 9888 ⓦ www.agapekeskus.ee 🕐 10.00–14.00 Mon–Thur

Eliisabeti Kirik (Eliisabeti Church)
This historic 18th-century church, with its lovely interior, is also one of Pärnu's favoured concert venues. ⓐ Nikolai 22 ☏ 443 1381 ⓦ www.eliisabet.ee

🔽 *Plenty of summer fun on the beach in Parnu*

THE ESTONIAN PLAYGROUND

Pärnu is where Estonians, especially from Tallinn, come to play and relax during the long days of summer. If you fancy joining them check out the opportunities below:

Bowling

Tervise Paradiis Spa Hotel & Water Park This large recreation complex was opened in 2004 and includes not just bowling but a host of other amenities, including a two-storey water park.
ⓐ Side 14 ⓣ 445 1616 ⓦ www.terviseparadiis.ee ⓛ 12.00–00.00 Mon–Thur & Sun, 11.00–01.00 Fri & Sat

Canoe trips

Edela Loodusmatkad Gentle canoeing adventures, either on slow-moving rivers or on the rapids on River Pärnu.
ⓐ Pärnade pst. 11, Paikuse ⓣ 525 1113 ⓦ www.loodusmatkad.ee
Fluvius kanuumatkad A chance to explore and view the scenery from the water. ⓣ 504 3670 ⓦ www.kanuuretked.ee

Golf

Golf is relatively new to Estonia, but demand has produced a host of good courses. Two of the best are:
Estonian Golf & Country Club This brand new course is called a country club but is also open to the public. It has two courses, the newest Stone Course and the slightly older Sea Course, which has grand fairways running along the sea.
ⓐ Manniva near Jõelähtme ⓣ 602 5290 ⓦ www.egcc.ee
ⓛ 08.00–20.00

Tallinn Golf Club Also known as Niitvälja, Estonia's oldest golf course is a favourite for many, given its proximity to Tallinn. Less challenging than Estonian Golf & Country Club. ⓐ Keila parish ❶ 678 0454 ⓦ www.egk-golf.ee

Two slightly easier courses are
Audru Golf ⓐ Audru Golf, Jõõpre, Audru vald ❶ 505 9868 ⓦ www.audrugolf.com
Valgeranna Golf ⓐ Villa Andropoff, Valgeranna, Audru vald ❶ 444 3453

Hiking
Maria talu This farm has a camping area, with horse riding and organised hikes. ⓐ Kõpu küla, Tõstamaa vald ❶ 447 4558/523 6066 ⓦ www.maria.ee
Tolli Tourism Farm Another farm, this one on Kinhu island, offering hiking and camping packages. ⓐ Sääre küla, Kihnu vald ❶ 527 7380 ⓦ www.kihnutalu.ee

Horse riding
Maria talu Campsite and hiking centre (see above) offering various horse riding options.
Riisa rantso A touch of Western style, for riding lessons and for horse trekking. ⓐ Riisa küla, Tori vald ❶ 510 0832 ⓦ www.riisarantso.ee
Tori stud Horse riding plus sightseeing trips in horse-drawn wagons at the stables where they breed the good-natured and elegant Tori horse. In winter, wagons are replaced by sledges

to get you through the snow. @ Pärnu mnt. 10 ❶ 522 6538
Ⓦ www.torihobune.ee

Saunas
Pühamüristus Offering a floating sauna and smoke sauna as
well as the usual options. @ Saarisoo, Jõesuu ❶ 506 1896
Ⓦ www.soomaa.com
Tori kanuumatkad @ Põrguwärk Tori ❶ 511 4253
Ⓦ www.tori.ee

Spas
See Spas outside Tallinn, page 136

Endla Teater (Endla Theatre)

This theatre is one of the town's major cultural centres, hosting
all manner of events. There's also an on-site café and gallery.
@ Keskväljak 1 ❶ 442 0666 Ⓦ www.endla.ee

Pärnu Kontserdisaal (Pärnu Concert Hall)

Right next to the river, this concert venue, the biggest in Pärnu,
hosts international names when they come to town. @ Aida 4
❶ 445 5800 Ⓦ www.concert.ee

Pärnu Muuseum (Pärnu Museum)

This museum covers 11,000 years of local history, from the
mid-Stone Age to the present. @ Aia 4 ❶ 443 3231 Ⓦ www.pernau.ee
🕒 10.00–18.00 Tues–Sat. Admission charge

Raekoda (Town Hall)

The Town Hall stages concerts and other events throughout summer. It's a particularly lovely place to hear classical music.
ⓐ Uus 4/Nikolai 3 ☎ 443 1405

Teatri Galerii (Theatre Gallery)

This building houses not only the town's largest drama theatre but also an art exhibition space. ⓐ Keskväljak 1 ☎ 442 0666
ⓦ www.endla.ee 🕐 11.00–17.00 Mon–Fri

Uue Kunsti Muuseum (Museum of New Art/Chaplin Centre)

Named after Charlie Chaplin, this cultural centre is housed in a former Communist Party HQ. ⓐ Esplanaadi 10 ☎ 443 0772
ⓦ www.chaplin.ee 🕐 09.00–21.00

RETAIL THERAPY

Port Artur A useful shopping centre with a supermarket, banks and various other services. ⓐ Hommiku 4 ☎ 447 8888 ⓦ www.portartur.ee
🕐 10.00–20.00 Mon–Sat, 10.00–18.00 Sun

Rüütli tänav (Knight Street) For a touch more individualism in the town's main shopping area, wander this street.

TAKING A BREAK

Chaplin Centre Café £ The café in the lobby of the cultural centre is a popular and cheap meeting place. ⓐ Esplanaadi 10 ☎ 443 0772
ⓦ www.chaplin.ee 🕐 09.00–21.00

Cibus £ Just next to the bus station, this bakery/café provides some of the freshest cookies and cakes available. ⓐ Ringi 3 ① 443 0117 ⓦ www.pereleib.ee ① 07.30–18.30 Mon–Fri, 07.30–16.00 Sat, 09.00–16.00 Sun

Sõõrikubaar £ This café-bakery is particularly famous for its *sõõrikud* (Estonian doughnuts). ⓐ Pühavaimu 15 ① 444 5334 ① 07.30–20.00 Mon–Sat, 09.00–17.00 Sun

Kadri £–££ A friendly, long-established restaurant serving traditional Estonian cuisine at low prices. ⓐ Nikolai 12 ① 442 9782 ① 07.30–21.00 Mon–Fri, 09.00–21.00 Sat, 09.00–18.00 Sun

Mõnus Margarita ££ This restaurant has won all the Estonian awards for its pleasant atmosphere and service. The food is Mexican, but if you're accustomed to spicy food ask the chef to make it hot. ⓐ Akadeemia 5 ① 443 0929 ⓦ www.servitris.ee ① 11.30–22.00 Mon & Sun, 11.30–23.00 Tues–Thur, 11.30–00.30 Fri & Sat

AFTER DARK

RESTAURANTS
Strand £ If you have a big appetite, bring it to the restaurant at the Strand Hotel. Both breakfast and dinner are buffet style. ⓐ Tammsaare pst. 35 ① 447 5370 ⓦ www.strand.ee ① 12.00–22.00 Sun–Thur, 12.00–23.00 Fri & Sat

Kuursaal £–££ Estonia's biggest tavern, the historic, 1890s-era Kuursaal near the beach, is also a venue for events. A popular stop for beachgoers looking for just a snack or one of the 'big bellyful'

meals. ⓐ Mere pst. 22 ⓣ 442 0367 Ⓦ www.kuur.ee ⓛ 18.00–02.00
Thur, 18.00–04.00 Fri & Sat

Café Grand ££ When it opened its doors in 1927, the Café attracted
the cream of the local society. It has live music on Friday and Saturday
nights. ⓐ Kuninga 25 ⓣ 444 3412 Ⓦ www.victoriahotel.ee
ⓛ 11.00–22.00

● *Wander through the pedestrianised shopping streets*

Seegi Maja ££–£££ The surroundings will make you think you have stepped back into the 17th century. Feast on items that might have graced the plate of Peter the Great (freshly made, of course). ⓐ Hospidali 1 ⓣ 443 0550 ⓦ www.seegimaja.ee ⓛ 12.00–22.00 Wed–Sun

Ammende Villa £££ Impressive Jugenstil building that serves as a high-class hotel and award-winning restaurant. Enjoy French and Mediterranean cuisine in the candlelit restaurant, or just go for a coffee on the sunny terrace. ⓐ Mere pst. 7 ⓣ 447 3888 ⓦ www.ammende.ee ⓛ 12.00–23.00

BAR

Kadunud Lootus This simple pub, whose name translates rather poignantly to 'Lost Hope Pub', fills up quickly with locals. ⓐ Tallinna mnt. 12 ⓣ 447 2119 ⓛ 12.00–00.00 Fri, 12.00–02.00 Sat–Thur

ACCOMMODATION

Freven Villa £ This is a historic residence of Pärnu with a tiny reception desk around the back. Rooms have their own toilets and there's a generous back garden for guests' use. Wi-Fi and bicycle rental, too. ⓐ Kooli 31 ⓣ 444 1540 or 566 86545 ⓦ www.freven.ee

Hommiku Hostel £ More like a small hotel than a hostel, Hommiku has singles, doubles and rooms for three or four people. All have their own shower/WC, TV and kitchenette (except the singles), plus internet access. The Old Town location is a further draw. ⓐ Hommiku 17 ⓣ 445 1122 ⓦ www.hommikuhostel.ee

Konse Holiday Village £ A combination of a guesthouse and caravan park, Konse is a winner. Rooms are basic but clean, and showers/WCs are shared. There are 50 caravan slots, plus all the necessary facilities. Bikes, boats and jet-skis can also be hired. ⓐ Suur-Jõe 44A ❶ 53 435 092 Ⓦ www.konse.ee

Carolina ££ Opened in 2006, this is in a modern building near the yacht harbour. Rooms are large and well equipped. ⓐ Ringi 54B ❶ 442 0440 Ⓦ www.carolina.ee

Delfine ££ On the street that leads to the beach, Delfine offers stylish rooms and suites, with facilities such as Wi-Fi. Massages and facials are offered in the beauty salon, and the restaurant is highly regarded. ⓐ Supeluse 22 ❶ 442 6900 Ⓦ www.delfine.ee

Green Villa ££ It's hard to miss the bright green exterior of this restored 1930s villa. The historic interior is attractive, with fireplaces and original hardwood floors. The guest rooms are comfy. ⓐ Vee 21 ❶ 443 6040 Ⓦ www.greenvilla.ee

Hotel Pärnu ££ A comfortable hotel close to the beach. Many rooms have lovely views over the town. Rates include breakfast and use of the sauna. ⓐ Rüütli 44 ❶ 447 8911 Ⓦ www.pergohotels.ee

Jahisadama Guesthouse ££ Right on the banks of the river, this has 18 brightly decorated rooms, each with its own shower and toilet. Staff can arrange extras such as boat rental and sauna sessions. ⓐ Lootsi 6 ❶ 447 1740 Ⓦ www.jahisadam.ee

Kanali Villa ££ This low-key, family-run hotel is in a quiet residential neighbourhood. All rooms have a shower and WC, while suites come with their own small kitchen. ⓐ Kanali 8 ⓣ 442 5846 ⓦ www.kanali.ee

Koidulapark Hotel ££ This building, dating from 1905, has been lovingly restored and turned into a 39-room hotel. Most of the features are new, but the feel is traditional. Wonderful views over the nearby park. ⓐ Kuninga 38 ⓣ 447 7030 ⓦ www.koidulaparkhotell.ee ⓛ Open Apr–Oct only

Promenaadi ££ A beautiful, painted wooden villa, built in 1905, on a quiet, leafy avenue. The brightly decorated rooms offer cable TV, fridge and their own shower/WC, and the location, close to both the city centre and Ranna Beach, is hard to beat. Breakfast not included. ⓐ Tammsaare pst.16 ⓣ 56 617 623 ⓦ www.promenaadi.net

Rähni Guesthouse ££ Each of the lovely rooms comes with a computer, printer, cable TV and fridge. There are also three apartments suitable for families. ⓐ Rähni 9 ⓣ 443 6222 ⓦ www.delfine.ee

Sadama Villa ££ This villa dates back to the 1930s but was only recently converted into a hotel. It's close to both the city centre and the harbour area, with cheery bedrooms and a garden to relax in. ⓐ Sadama 13 ⓣ 447 0008 ⓦ www.sadamavilla.ee

Villa Ene ££ This cosy guesthouse is just a few minutes' walk from the town centre. Rooms come with their own shower and toilet, satellite TV, fridge and coffee maker. Breakfast isn't provided. ⓐ Auli 10a ⓣ 442 5532 ⓦ www.villaene.ee

Alex Maja £££ Set in a little courtyard in the middle of downtown, this attractive hotel features decent-sized rooms with cheery décor. ⓐ Kuninga 20 ⓣ 446 1866 ⓦ www.alexmaja.ee

Ammende Villa £££ One of the best choices in this category, this impressive art nouveau building, surrounded by gardens, dates from 1905. The antiques-filled rooms are luxurious (those in the Gardener's House are plainer), and the suites are worth the extra. Splurge on dinner in the fine-dining restaurant, and enjoy classical music performances in the garden or the salon on Thursdays. ⓐ Mere pst. 7 ⓣ 447 3888 ⓦ www.ammende.ee

Scandic Hotel Rannahotell £££ The Rannahotell dates from 1937, when the Pärnu Beach was a magnet for beachgoers from all over Europe. Architecturally, the hotel is the epitome of Estonian functionalism. The restaurant is worth a stop in any season, though it's ideal in summertime, when the large terrace is open. ⓐ Ranna pst. 5 ⓣ 443 2950 ⓦ www.scandic-hotels.ee

St Peterburg £££ If a hotel can be a monument to the era of Peter the Great, then this is it. Everything is decorated as if it were from Peter's time, and the hotel has a wine cellar that the Tsar himself might have liked. ⓐ Hospidali 6 ⓣ 443 0555 ⓦ www.seegimaja.ee

Victoria £££ The Victoria is a Pärnu institution. It's not only an excellent hotel, it's also a great place to have a quiet meal. Take tea in the parlour and feel like royalty. The Victoria hasn't been able to completely duck progress – it has Wi-Fi throughout. ⓐ Kuninga 25 ⓣ 444 3412 ⓦ www.victoriahotel.ee

Tartu

The first written records of Tartu date from 1030. Now the second-largest city in Estonia, it lies 185 km (115 miles) southeast of Tallinn. It is known as a vibrant university town with a rich cultural heritage. In addition to Tartu University, founded in 1632, there is the Estonian Agricultural Academy and the Tartu Defence College. The city is also known for its research institutions, which represent most fields of science. The Emajõgi River flows through Tartu, adding colour to the city.

● *The Emajõgi River runs through Tartu*

GETTING THERE

Tartu can be reached by car from the capital by following Tartu maantee (Highway 2). Frequent, regular bus services run between the two cities, with a journey time of two and a half hours for the express services.

The **Tourist Information Centre** (ⓐ Raekoda ⓣ 744 2111 ⓦ www.visittartu.com ⓛ 09.00–18.00 Mon–Fri, 10.00–17.00 Sat, 10.00–15.00 Sun, mid-May–mid-Sept; 09.00–17.00 Mon–Fri, 10.00–15.00 Sat, mid-Sept–mid-May) in Tartu is a full-service affair, providing travel tips on all of southern Estonia. Here, staff will arrange guides and book accommodation; there's also an internet terminal.

CITY OF GOOD THOUGHTS

Tartu calls itself the 'City of Good Thoughts', which is interesting when you consider it has so frequently been burnt to the ground by advancing and retreating armies. Tartu is the home of Estonia's finest university and, as everyone knows, university students make a town special. Rather than rush from place to place in Tartu, it's best to simply wander and see what grabs your eye. If you're lucky enough to be there for more than a day, visit the Supilinn neighbourhood. What used to be a district of ramshackle wooden houses is being reborn into what could become one of the country's great neighbourhoods. You'll find plenty of good thoughts coming from that area of the city.

SIGHTS & ATTRACTIONS

19. sajandi Tartu Linnakodaniku Muuseum (19th-century Tartu Citizen's Home)

Providing a fascinating glimpse of what Tartu life was like in the early 19th century, this re-created middle-class dwelling from the 1830s is decorated with Biedermeier furniture. Detailed explanations in English help set the tone. ③ Jaani 16 ⓣ 736 1545 ⓦ www.tartu.ee/linnamuuseum ⓛ 11.00–18.00 Wed–Sun, summer; 10.00–15.00 Wed–Sun, winter. Admission charge

Cathedral ruins

The huge red brick structure at the northwest tip of the hill is the remains of the 13th-century Dome Cathedral. It was heavily damaged

⬤ *The massive Cathedral ruins*

during the Livonian War and finally destroyed by fire in 1624. Today, it houses the University History Museum (see page 125).

Inglisild (Angel's Bridge)
Want to make your dreams come true? Hold your breath as you go across it, and make a wish.

Jaani Kirik (St John's Church)
This 14th-century building is Tartu's oldest surviving church. It was wrecked in World War II and stood derelict for nearly half a century, before being renovated, reconsecrated and, in 2005, reopened to the public. Inside and outside the church are around 1,000 terracotta figures. ⓐ Jaani 5 ⓣ 744 2229 ⓦ www.jaanikirik.ee ⓛ 10.00–18.00 Tues–Sat

Kuradisild (Devil's Bridge)
Just past the Church of the Virgin Mary, the Devil's Bridge was built in 1913 to honour the 300th anniversary of Romanov rule in Russia.

Pauluse Kirik (St Paul's Church)
This towering church, with its distinctively square copper spire, is unlike the city's other churches as it was built by Finnish architect Eliel Saarinen in 1917. Worth a visit for a glance at its bright, art nouveau interior. ⓐ Riia 27 ⓣ 742 0258 ⓦ www.eelk.ee/tartu.pauluse ⓛ 10.00–17.00 Mon–Fri, 10.00–14.00 Sat, 09.00–12.00 Sun

Peetri Kirik (St Peter's Church)
Fans of all forms of Gothic ecclesiastical architecture will be fascinated by this structure whose primary point of interest is a two-storey nave that's surrounded by ornate chandeliers. The fact that this church

regularly welcomes a couple of thousand worshippers is testament
to many Estonians' strong religious faith. ⓐ Narva mnt. 104
ⓣ 733 3261 ⓛ 10.00–14.00 Tues–Sat, closed Sun after service

Püha Suurkannataja Georgi (Jüri) (Church of St George the Conqueror)

This pretty pink Russian Orthodox church was originally built in 1870,
then reconsecrated in 1945 after post-war restoration. If possible, try
to look inside at the elaborate icons. ⓐ Narva mnt. 105 ⓛ 09.00–14.00

Pühima Neitsi Maarja Pärispatuta Saamise (Church of the Virgin Mary)

Built in 1899, this is a wonderful example of late 19th-century,
neo-historicist architecture. The vaulted interior with stained-glass
windows is well worth a look. The altar painting *Virgin Mary with
Jesus* dates from 1905. ⓐ Veski 1a ⓣ 742 2731 ⓦ www.neitsimaarja.ee
ⓛ 09.00–11.00, 17.00–20.00 Mon–Fri, 09.00–10.00, 18.00–19.00
Sat, 09.00–14.00 Sun

Raekoda (Town Hall)

The striking pink building looming over Town Hall Square is Tartu's
Town Hall. Built in 1789 by the town's master builder, Johann Heinrich
Bartholomäus Walter, it mixes early classicism with baroque and rococo,
and is the third Town Hall to have stood on this spot, after the first two
were destroyed by fire. In its day, the cellar and the ground floor on the
left side housed a prison, while the right side was a weigh house. Today,
the building serves as the city's administrative centre. The 18-bell
carillon rings every day at 12.00 and 18.00. ⓐ Raekoja plats ⓣ 731 1101

Sacrificial Stone & Kissing Hill

The huge stone here marks just one of the several hundred
pagan sites in Estonia. It is thought to have had some relevance

to fertility. Kissing Hill – the place to which local newly-weds are supposed to repair for some quality nuptial time after the brouhaha of the ceremonials – continues that theme.

CULTURE

A Le Coq Õllemuuseum (A Le Coq Beer Museum)
On the A Le Coq brewery tour you get a glimpse of the mostly automated process by which the company cranks out 40 million litres (9 million gallons) of beer every year. Most of the tour is spent in the beer museum, set in the old malt-drying tower that was still in operation until 1997. The exhibition starts with the beer-making culture of the ancient Sumerians and moves on to show equipment used in this factory since it started up in 1879. And, yes, you do get a sample at the end. ⓐ Tähtvere 56/62 ⓣ 744 9711 ⓦ www.alecoq.ee ⓛ Tours: 14.00 Thur, 10.00, 12.00 & 14.00 Sat. Admission charge

KGB Kongid (KGB Cells Museum)
The KGB Cells Museum is housed in Tartu's infamous 'Grey House', which was the regional KGB headquarters in the 1940s and 1950s. Apart from the lock-ups themselves, the museum has extensive exhibits here on deportations, life in the gulags and Estonian resistance movements. ⓐ Riia 15b (entrance from Pepleri) ⓣ 746 1717 ⓦ www.tartu.ee/linnamuuseum ⓛ 11.00–16.00 Tues–Sat. Admission charge

Luudusmuuseum (Natural History Museum)
Although this museum does contain a nice collection of minerals in the corridor, most of the display is taken up by hundreds and hundreds of fossils – mainly small marine animals, but also primates and a

◔ *Tartu's pretty pink Town Hall*

few mammoth bits from Siberia. In a separate zoology section is a collection of stuffed animals containing everything from mice to giraffes. If you're not squeamish, check out the 'rat king' – 13 rats who went about their business with their tails knotted together. This rare find was discovered on a farm in Võru county in early 2005. ⓐ Vanemuise 46 ❶ 737 5839 Ⓦ www.ut.ee/BGGM ⏰ 10.00–16.00 Wed–Sun. Admission charge

Mänguasjamuuseum (Tartu Toy Museum)

This museum, popular with adults as well as their offspring, displays everything from antique paper pop-ups to electric train sets. ⓐ Lutsu 8 ❶ 746 1777 Ⓦ www.mm.ee ⏰ 11.00–18.00 Wed–Sun. Admission charge

Tartu Laululava (Tartu Song Festival Arena)

This arena (which looks like a huge clam shell) was built specifically to house the many festivals that celebrate Estonians' passionate love of song, which is intrinsic to their culture and was even the catalyst for the 'Singing Revolution' (see page 21). If you do happen to be visiting when one is occurring, you'll be exhilarated by performances given, especially those of entrants to the students' competition. ⓐ Laulupeo 25 ❶ 742 2108 Ⓦ www.arena.ee

Tartu Lennundusmuuseum (Tartu Aviation Museum)

Some of the home-produced exhibits in this museum are a fascinating reminder that, not so very long ago, Estonians were part of a huge and sophisticated system of thought whose ideology was so opposed to the West's that they were armed to the teeth in case the two cultures descended into war. In today's vastly different climate, visitors may inspect the huge range of aeronautical items

on display here (and we're talking everything from models to fully operational fighter jets) at their leisure, without resorting to furtive hidden camera work. ⓐ Veskiorg 1, Lange ☎ 502 6712 Ⓦ www.lennundusmuuseum.ee 🕐 10.00–18.00. Admission charge

Tartu Linnamuuseum (Tartu City Museum)

The best overview of Tartu's history can be found at the City Museum, housed in a beautiful, 18th-century mansion just across the river from the Old Town. The collection isn't terribly extensive, but all the major periods are covered. Don't miss the computer-generated video that shows what medieval Tartu would have looked like. ⓐ Narva mnt. 23 ☎ 746 1911 Ⓦ www.tartu.ee/linnamuuseum 🕐 11.00–18.00 Wed–Sun. Admission charge

Tartu Theatre Laboratory

As with all theatrical 'laboratories', 'spaces' and 'exchanges', you should steel yourself for experimentalism before you visit. ⓐ Lutsu 2 ☎ 5349 9811

Tartu Ülikooli Ajaloo Muuseum (Tartu University History Museum)

Part of the Dome Cathedral is now a multi-storey museum detailing the history of Tartu University from its founding in 1632 to the present day. Everything from old laboratory equipment to student life is featured. The beautiful old library is well worth a look. ⓐ Lossi 25 ☎ 737 5674 Ⓦ www.ut.ee/ajaloomuuseum 🕐 11.00–17.00 Wed–Sun. Admission charge

Tartu Ülikooli & Kunstimuuseum (Tartu University & Art Museum)

This grand neoclassical structure was built in 1809 for the reopening of Tartu University. Inside, the University Art Museum houses a collection of classical sculptures, as well as a mummy from the 2nd millennium BC. Unfortunately, most of the sculptures here are plaster copies, as the originals were taken to Russia during World War II.

At the museum you can get tickets to see the fabulously decorated Aula (Assembly Hall), and the building's most interesting feature, the Student Lock-up, where, in the 19th century, students were incarcerated for minor offences. Cartoons and graffiti still cover the walls. ⓐ Ülikooli 18 ⓣ 737 5384 ⓦ www.ut.ee ⓛ 11.00–17.00 Mon–Fri. Admission charge

Vanemuine Teater (Theatre Vanemuine/Big House)
This was established in 1870, and may well be the country's oldest still-operative theatre. There are actually three stages here (the Big House is complemented by the Little House and the Port Theatre), and many varieties of performance take place. ⓐ Vanemuise 6 ⓣ 744 0165 ⓦ www.vanemuine.ee

Vanemuise Kontserdisaal (Vanemuise Concert Hall)
This is Tartu's leading entertainments venue, and thus stages some high-profile, high-quality events. ⓐ Vanemuise 6 ⓣ 737 7530 ⓦ www.concert.ee ⓛ Box office: 09.00–17.00 Mon–Fri & 1 hr before performances

Viltune Maja & Tartu Kunstimuuseum (Leaning House & Tartu Art Museum)
Estonia's 'Leaning House' – or Barclay House as it's officially called – stands in Town Hall Square. Builders in the 1790s unwisely set part of its foundation on the old city wall and another part on wooden piles. The latter eventually sank, giving the house its discernable lean. Thankfully, it was saved from collapse by Polish engineers,

◔ *Tartu University's campus has endless charm*

who shored it up during the Soviet period. It now hosts Tartu's worthwhile Art Museum. ⓐ Raekoja plats 18 ⓣ 744 1080 ⓦ www.tartmus.ee ⓛ 11.00–18.00 Wed–Sun. Admission charge

RETAIL THERAPY

Antoniuse Courtyard All the products of Estonia's folk and traditional crafts – whether they're things that adorn your table, your bed, your ankles or your earlobes – are for sale here; and you can observe craftspeople in action, too. ⓐ Lutsu 5 ⓣ 742 3823 ⓦ www.antonius.ee ⓛ 12.00–18.00

TAKING A BREAK

Kapriis £ A modest café-bar with an interesting design, right in the centre of town. It offers a simple menu and good-value daily specials. ⓐ Raekoja plats 9 ⓣ 734 1166 ⓦ www.kapriis.ee ⓛ 11.00–22.00 Mon, 11.00–00.00 Tues, Wed & Sun, 11.00–01.00 Thur, 11.00–02.00 Fri & Sat

Kondiitriäri £ This café knows all about the international lure of the aroma of pastries baked freshly on the premises. Leave your calorie counter outside. ⓐ Rüütli 5 ⓣ 740 0366 ⓦ www.pereleib.ee ⓛ 07.30–19.00 Mon–Fri, 08.00–16.00 Sat, 10.00–17.00 Sun

Moka £ Offers a vast choice of cakes and pies at low prices – thus attracting students from the local university. ⓐ Küütri 3 ⓣ 744 2085 ⓦ www.moka.ee ⓛ 10.30–23.00 Mon–Thur, 10.30–00.00 Fri, 11.30–00.00 Sat, 11.30–21.00 Sun

Opera Pizza £ The clue to the fare on offer here is suggested in the name – this is very much the place to come if you want to plunge your fangs into an Estonian pizza. ⓐ Vanemuise 26 ⓣ 742 0795 ⓛ 11.00–21.00 Sun–Thur, 11.00–22.00 Fri & Sat

Café Truffe £–££ French-style café with a slightly bohemian atmosphere. You can't beat the hot chocolate with marshmallows for livening up a cold winter afternoon. ⓐ Raekoja plats 16 ⓣ 742 8840 ⓦ www.truffe.ee ⓛ 11.00–23.00 Mon–Thur, 11.00–01.00 Fri & Sat, 11.00–22.00 Sun

Crepp £–££ Once again, the clue's in this Old Town favourite's name: Crepp celebrates the crêpe, alongside a host of other French dishes bang in the middle of Tartu. The ideal place to debut that beret you've never had the nerve to wear at home. ⓐ Rüütli 16 ⓣ 552 8170 ⓦ www.crepp.ee ⓛ 11.00–00.00 Sun–Thur, 11.00–01.00 Fri & Sat

AFTER DARK

RESTAURANTS

Big Ben ££ This is Tartu's English-style eaterie, and, like such places right across the planet, it majors in fish and chips, bread and butter and sausages and mash. So, if you need a bit of home-comfort noshing, get yourself down to this friendly restaurant with all haste. ⓐ Riia 4 ⓣ 730 2662 ⓦ www.bigbenpub.ee ⓛ 07.00–01.00 Tues–Thur, 07.00–02.00 Fri, 08.00–02.00 Sat, 08.00–00.00 Sun

Suudlevad Tudengid (The Kissing Students) ££ A lovely name for a lovely restaurant, which boasts its own in-house pub. This tends to be the meeting place for the denizens of Tartu's bridge-playing community, so you'll be more than welcome if you fancy a game. ⓐ Raekoja plats 10 ⓣ 730 1893 ⓦ www.suudlevadtudengid.ee ⓛ 11.00–00.00 Mon & Sun, 11.00–01.00 Tues–Thur, 11.00–03.00 Fri & Sat

Atlantis £££ This is probably *the* restaurant to visit in Tartu right now. It's posh and it's precious, but it isn't pretentious, and you can sample Estonian specialities in style. ⓐ Narva mnt. 2 ⓣ 738 5495 ⓦ www.atlantis.ee ⓛ 12.00–00.00 Sun–Thur, 12.00–01.00 Fri & Sat

Barclay £££ The Barclay Hotel has the (some would say dubious) distinction of having been the Red Army's HQ in the 50 years preceding independence. The restaurant has moved seamlessly into the new way of doing things by relying on the sheer quality of its service and fare (modern Estonian). A place in which to indulge yourself. ⓐ Ülikooli 8 ⓣ 744 7100 ⓦ www.barclay.ee ⓛ 07.00–23.00 Mon–Fri, 08.00–23.00 Sat & Sun

Püssirohu Kelder £££ This restaurant contradicts those who would deny that you can have a slap-up meal in a former munitions dump. The chef is justly renowned for the miracles he can perform with a salmon. ⓐ Lossi 28 ⓣ 730 3555 ⓦ www.pyss.ee ⓛ 12.00–02.00 Mon–Thur, 12.00–03.00 Fri & Sat, 12.00–00.00 Sun

Volga £££ Tartu's most exclusive restaurant, legendary already from Soviet times but now completely renovated and catering for upper-class tie-wearing diners. Their romantic dance nights are worth attending. ⓐ Küütri 1 ⓣ 730 5444 ⓦ www.restaurantvolga.ee ⓛ 18.00–23.00 Mon–Fri, 12.00–00.00 Sat

Werner £££ Just up the stairs of the café of the same name, this is

a classy establishment whose gentleman's club ambience seems to repel and attract in equal measure. ⓐ Ülikooli 11 ⓣ 742 6377 ⓦ www.werner.ee ⓛ 07.30–23.00 Mon–Thur, 08.00–01.00 Fri & Sat, 09.00–21.00 Sun

CLUBS & BARS

Gläm The restaurant offers a glamorous mix of Chinese, Thai and Nepalese cuisine, bul it's best to come on weekend nights, when the place turns into a club where you can party until the early hours. ⓐ Kompanii 2 ⓣ 744 1185 ⓦ www.glam.ee ⓛ 11.00–23.00 Mon–Thur, 11.00–03.00 Fri, 12.00–01.00 Sat, 12.00–22.00 Sun

🔺 *Take a break in Tartu's cobbled Old Town*

Illegaard Jazz Club This club runs the jazz gamut, right back to Dixieland. ⓐ Ülikooli 5 ⓣ 518 4999 ⓒ 14.00–04.00 Mon–Fri, 12.00–04.00 Sat & Sun

Krooks It's definitely heavy on the metal at this gathering place for Tartu's born to be wild crowd. Denim rock is worshipped without so much as a blush here, and you'll find a hearty welcome from the head-banging patrons. ⓐ Jakobi 34 ⓣ 744 1506 ⓦ www.krooks.ee ⓒ 11.00–04.30

Õlle Tare It's hearty slaps on the back, vats of lager downed in one and the jaunty sound of the oompah-pah band at this German-themed boozeria. Whether you've got the legs for *lederhosen* or not, you'll have a wild old time here. ⓐ Aleksandri 42 ⓣ 734 4766 ⓦ www.olletare.ee ⓒ 12.00–17.00 Mon, 12.00–01.00 Tues–Wed, 12.00–02.00 Thur, 12.00–03.00 Fri & Sat. Admission charge after 22.00 Thur–Sat

Place Beer Colors Notable mainly for its décor – mechanical spinning legs dangle from the ceiling and occasionally spring into action – this is a fantastic spot for relaxing in the company of a student crowd who now can't actually remember the Soviet days. ⓐ Küüni 2 ⓣ 744 1438 ⓦ www.bcplace.ee ⓒ 11.00–00.00 Mon–Thur, 11.00–02.00 Fri & Sat, 12.00–23.00 Sun

Shakespeare It was a generous move for the land of Madis Kõiv to name a club after the Bard. Beyond the resonance of the name, this is notable for the music-and-speech recitals that occur frequently here. ⓐ Vanemuise 6 ⓣ 744 0140 ⓦ www.shakespeare.ee ⓒ 11.00–23.00 Sun–Thur, 11.00–01.00 Fri & Sat

Ülikooli Kohvik This is a hangout of the self-consciously intellectual students, so don't be surprised if you take your cake and coffee to the accompaniment of an incomprehensible, high-volume academic debate. But the verbal parry and thrust is always good-natured, and so the atmosphere benefits. ⓐ Ülikooli 20 ⓣ 737 5405 ⓦ www.kohvik.ut.ee
ⓒ 1st floor: 07.30–19.00 Mon–Fri, 10.00–16.00 Sat & Sun; 2nd floor: 11.00–23.00 Mon–Thur, 11.00–01.00 Fri & Sat, 11.00–21.00 Sun

ACCOMMODATION

Starest £ The big selling point of this hostel is the satellite telly on offer. That said, the rooms are particularly pretty and the beds are comfy. ⓐ Mõisavahe 21 ⓣ 740 0674 ⓦ www.starest.ee

Tartu Hostel £ This central hostel – actually University halls of residence – has got the lot, from an in-house juice bar to Wi-Fi connection for your laptop. There is a sister hostel with much the same facilities at Narva mnt. 27. ⓐ Pepleri 14 ⓣ 742 7608
ⓦ www.tartuhostel.eu

Park ££ The atmosphere of this charismatic, 1940s-built hotel is one of a sort of film-noir laconic wistfulness. Rooms are perfectly comfortable and the staff are friendly. ⓐ Vallikraavi 23 ⓣ 742 7000
ⓦ www.parkhotell.ee

Tartu ££ At last: somewhere you would recognise as having a cheery hostel ambience. That's in no sense meant to be derogatory, as all facilities here are perfectly adequate.
ⓐ Soola 3 ⓣ 731 4300 ⓦ www.tartuhotell.ee

Vikerkaare ££ If you want extremely quiet and extremely safe, you should consider this guesthouse, which is right in the middle of an otherwise residential area. 🅐 Vikerkaare 40 ☎ 742 1190 🅦 www.hot.ee/tdc

Draakon £££ If your mantra is location, location, location, then this hotel triumphs because it's central, central, central. That's far from all, though, and the bathrooms are of palatial proportions. 🅐 Raekoja plats 2 ☎ 744 2045 🅦 www.draakon.ee

Hansa Hotell £££ Tartu's historic, Hanseatic credentials are exploited with great taste here, and the resulting 'olde worlde' atmosphere is beautifully complemented by the Emajõgi River, which flows just behind the hotel. 🅐 Aleksandri 46 ☎ 737 1800 🅦 www.hansahotell.ee

London £££ This classy establishment offers modern facilities in an historical part of town. Rooms are nicely decorated in a Finnish style, and the London gets a particular thumbs-up for its disability-friendly approach. 🅐 Rüütli 9 ☎ 730 5555 🅦 www.londonhotel.ee

Uppsala Maja £££ Tartu has many quaint buildings, and this 250-year-old wooden construction is chief among them. Rooms are perhaps a shade small, but each one is cosy and personable. Take some photos: your friends back home will be envious. 🅐 Jaani 7 ☎ 736 1535 🅦 www.uppsalamaja.ee

Pallas £££+ The London's posh sister is one of Tartu's ritzier hotels. What makes it really stand out is its interior decoration, which is heavily influenced by the intricate beauty of the Pallas school of art (the most famous sometime-member of which was Gustav Klimt). 🅐 Riia mnt. 4 ☎ 730 1200 🅦 www.pallas.ee

Lahemaa National Park

GETTING THERE

The park lies around 70 km (44 miles) east of Tallinn, on Estonia's north coast. Buses do run from Tallinn's central bus station (see Ⓦ www.bussireisid.ee for bus times to Palmse) but these are slow and run at inconvenient times. Tour company **Orion Reisid** (ⓒ 631 0540 Ⓦ www.orionreisid.ee) offers day trips which include all transport, guides and picnic. To reach Lahemaa by car, take the E20 east out of the city, then turn left at Viitna towards Palmse.

Visitor Centre ⓐ Palmse, Lääne-Virumaa ⓒ 329 5555 Ⓦ www.lahemaa.ee ⓛ 09.00–19.00 summer; times vary in winter

SIGHTS & ATTRACTIONS

Lahemaa Rahvuspark (Lahemaa National Park)

Around two thirds of this 72,500 ha park on Estonia's wild north coast is covered with oak, birch, fir and pine trees, with the remaining third covered by sea. Lahemaa, which means 'Land of Bays', has been a national park since 1971 and is a site of immense biodiversity as well as natural beauty. Bears, wolves, lynx and wild boar all live in the densely forested areas, and the coastline is a paradise for birdwatchers with its masses of migratory waterfowl.

It's worth hiring a freelance guide to take you around, although trails are generally well-signed and maintained if you prefer to explore alone. You can hire guides and pick up maps at the Visitor Centre, which is housed in the beautifully restored 18th-century Palmse Manor, a converted distillery fronted by a swan-filled lake. There is a lovely café and you can watch a film entitled *Lahemaa – Nature and Man*.

Spas outside Tallinn

If you want to extend your city break and fancy a few days' relaxation or the chance to try indulgent beauty treatments, then why not head to a spa? Or you may think your health would benefit from professional treatment, medicine that will go down all the better when it also offers the chance to explore a little more of Estonia and the benefits of sea air. Tallinn has several spa hotels as well as a number of impressive day spas dotted around the country.

On offer are a range of programmes from pampering beauty treatments and massages to more invasive procedures – so do check these are appropriate with your own doctor before you travel. The cost of your stay will depend not only on the spa you choose – and on whether you stay the night or just visit for the day – but also on the treatments you opt for. Make sure you do some research before deciding. Most spas have websites which detail the packages they offer throughout the year.

HAAPSALU

Fra Mare Spa The question is: is it worth trekking 100 km (62 miles) from Tallinn to hit the Fra? Well, the apparently miraculous powers of its mud are renowned, and it offers such intriguing treatments as ear candling and the chocolate and/or red grape body wrap (there are worse ways of being mummified). The resort itself is absolutely beautiful and clinically hygienic. It's your shout, but we say go. ⓐ Ranna tee 2 ⓣ 472 4600 ⓦ www.framare.ee

⬥ *Choose from a variety of treatments in the spa towns around Tallinn*

ISLAND OF SAAREMAA

GO Spa Hotell 'GO' stands for Georg Ots, the famous Estonian crooner who was a massive hit in Russia. GO Spa is probably Estonia's most famous luxury spa and indeed may be the best. It offers the usual suspects (massage, body treatment, hydrotherapy, facials) but does it in a way which keeps customers coming back. Also, the spa cuisine is rather remarkable. ➌ Tori 2, Kuressaare, Saaremaa ➊ 455 0000 Ⓦ www.gospa.ee

PÄRNU

Estonia Spa This supersize complex seems to be forever expanding. Housed in three buildings, with the White House and the Green House connected by an elevated glass walkway, and the famous Pärnu Mudaravila, that beautiful, domed building near the beach. Each facility offers decent, hotel-style rooms and a full range of treatment options. Most guests arrive in large groups and convalesce here for a week, so it's best to book at least a month in advance. ➌ Tammsaare pst. 4A ➊ 447 6905 Ⓦ www.spaestonia.ee

Sõprus Health Rehabilitation Centre Some guests prefer to stay in the spa's classic yellow wooden villa, but, most are housed in the more modern adjacent building attached to the treatment centre. Rooms are all fully fitted out – some have balconies, and most have internet connections. ➌ Eha 2 ➊ 445 0790 Ⓦ www.spahotelsoprus.com

Tervise Paradiis The largest spa hotel in Estonia has seven buildings connected by glass galleries, which gives them a decidedly space-age look. A full range of therapies is available and rooms here rival those in Pärnu's best hotels. ⓐ Side 14 ⓣ 445 1600 ⓦ www.terviseparadiis.ee

Viiking Spa Hotel This attractive, modern sanatorium near the yacht harbour is also a fine hotel, a few steps ahead of others in town in terms of comfort. Healthy services run the whole gamut, from infrared sauna to honey massage. This is also one of Estonia's leading cardiac treatment centres, so don't worry about over-exerting yourself during your stay. ⓐ Sadama 15 ⓣ 443 1293 ⓦ www.viiking.ee

Villa Medica Pärnu's smallest sanatorium is in fact a private clinic specialising in the treatment of musculoskeletal problems, but it makes its hotel rooms available to both patients and non-patients alike. Day surgery, beauty treatments and massage are also available. ⓐ Tammsaare 39 ⓣ 442 7121 ⓦ www.villamedica.ee

EASTERN ESTONIA

Kalvi Manor On a first glance at this seaside manor house, you might think you were in England, so sumptuous is the structure and its gardens. It has every convenience the huntin', shootin' and fishin' set could possibly demand. ⓐ Near the village of Aseri, 100 km (62 miles) east of Tallinn ⓣ 339 5300 ⓦ www.kalvi-hotel.com

Saka Cliff Hotel and Spa The neo-Renaissance Saka Manor and the park surrounding it are situated on the limestone bank of northern Estonia, where the 1,200 km (746 miles) Baltic Klint reaches its highest point.

Spa services include a range of massage treatments and both infrared and steam sauna. ❸ Kohtla vald, Ida-Virumaa, about 160 km (100 miles) from Tallinn along the St Petersburg road ❶ 336 4900 ❿ www.saka.ee

Toila Spa Hotel This sanatorium offers a comprehensive range of treatments, and is particularly strong on electrotherapy, massage and saunas. It has two features that may well be unique: a 'Salt Chamber', an area whose salty atmosphere is reckoned to help various types of chest problems and breathing difficulties; and a 21st-centry version of a Roman spa ❸ Ranna 12, Toila ❶ 334 2900 ❿ www.toilaspa.ee

MUHU ISLAND

Pädaste Manor This late-medieval manor has become the kind of pan-facility hotel in which lottery winners are advised to seek refuge while they work out what they're going to do with their winnings. Core health-improving treatments include aromatherapy, hay baths and scrubs, and auxiliary treats include a restaurant and cinema. ❸ Muhu Island ❶ 454 8800 ❿ www.padaste.ee

▶ *Tallinn is the gateway port to Estonia*

PRACTICAL
information

Directory

GETTING THERE
By air
The easiest way to get to Tallinn is by air. Tallinn Lennart Meri Airport (see page 54) is modern and user-friendly. It is serviced by direct flights with **Estonian Air** (Ⓦ www.estonian-air.ee) from 16 cities in Europe, including London. **easyJet** (Ⓦ www.easyjet.com) flies to Tallinn from London Stansted. The airport has a full range of services, including currency exchange, banks and ATMs. It's wise to get some local currency before heading into town.

Many people are aware that air travel emits CO_2, which contributes to climate change. You may be interested in the possibility of lessening the environmental impact of your flight through the charity **Climate Care** (Ⓦ www.climatecare.org), which offsets your CO_2 by funding environmental projects around the world.

By rail
There is a direct service to Moscow in Russia, but no direct connections to the rest of Europe. In general, railway systems throughout the Baltic States are poor. The *Thomas Cook European Rail Timetable* has up-to-date schedules for European international and national train services.
Thomas Cook European Rail Timetable ❶ (UK) 01733 416477; (USA) 1 800 322 3834 Ⓦ www.thomascookpublishing.com

By road
Driving across Europe to Tallinn can take a long time, with the total distance from Calais being about 2,460 km (1,529 miles). The roads are good and fast through Western Europe, but once you reach

Poland the pace will slow, as there are few multi-lane highways in Poland and the Baltic States.

There is a regular bus service to Riga in Latvia and Vilnius, Lithuania, with connections to most other major European cities through **Eurolines** (W www.eurolines.com) and **Ecolines** (W www.ecolines.net),

▼ *Tallinn's train station*

who run services to Tallinn from a number of cities in Germany and Eastern Europe. **Hansabuss** (W www.businessline.ee) has recently added a new luxury bus service connecting Tallinn and Riga. Aimed at coaxing business travellers out from behind the wheels of their cars, it is twice the price of Eurolines but the comfort and convenience are doubled as well. The bus offers free Wi-Fi for the five-hour journey.

By water
The Port of Tallinn is located about 1 km (½ mile) northeast of the city centre. There are regular ferry and catamaran connections from Helsinki, operated mainly by Tallink, Viking Line and Nordic Jet Line, and a ferry service from Stockholm run by Tallink.
Port of Tallinn ☎ 631 8550 W www.ts.ee

ENTRY FORMALITIES
A valid passport is required to enter the country. Since Estonia joined the EU in 2004, entry into the country for most people has become very easy. Entry from another EU country is normally quick, while entry from Russia can take some time. Citizens of most countries do not require a visa unless they plan to stay longer than 90 days. Children aged seven to 15 years must have their own passport when travelling to Estonia unless they are registered in a parent's passport, in which case there should be a photo of the child next to the name. Children under seven years do not require a photo if they are registered in a parent's passport.

For more information or to check the visa status of your country, check the website of the **Estonian Ministry of Foreign Affairs** (W www.vm.ee).

There are some restrictions on the import of dairy products

and milk. The import of tobacco products, alcohol and prescription medicines is allowed, but the amount is limited. Customs information for Estonia is available at Ⓦ www.emta.ee

MONEY

The national currency is the Estonian kroon (kr.). One kroon equals approximately 0.06 euros. The kroon is broken down into 100 sents. There are coins of 10, 20 and 50 sents, and of 1 and 5kr. There are banknotes of 2, 5, 10, 25, 50, 100 and 500kr. Estonia plans to join the euro in 2013 at the earliest.

Traveller's cheques can be exchanged in banks, but are less likely to be accepted in shops. Eurocheque is the most widely accepted traveller's cheque, but American Express and Thomas Cook are also accepted. Most larger hotels, stores and restaurants take Visa, MasterCard, Eurocard, Diner's Club and American Express. Many shops and restaurants, especially those frequented by tourists, will accept euros. However, it is always advisable to carry Estonian kroons with you.

Banks and ATMs are plentiful and easy to find in Tallinn. Banks are open 09.00–18.00 Monday to Friday and occasionally on Saturday morning. All banks offer currency exchange. Exchange offices are also found in larger hotels, the airport, train station, ferry terminal and major shopping centres.

HEALTH, SAFETY & CRIME

Estonia is relatively safe in terms of health problems. No immunisations or health certificates are required before visiting. If you plan to hike in wooded or boggy areas, you should be vaccinated against tick-borne encephalitis. The tap water is safe to drink, although it may be less than palatable.

Minor ailments can usually be treated at pharmacies, which carry a wide range of international drugs, from painkillers to antibiotics. Pharmacies are normally open from 10.00 to 19.00, but one, **Tõnismäe apteek** (ⓐ Tõnismägi 5 ❶ 644 2282), is open 24 hours a day. It is located near the city centre.

Major complaints are best treated at a hospital (*haigla*). Emergency treatment is free, but if you are admitted to hospital, you will be charged a fee for bed space and drugs.

The standard of medical care is high, and most doctors speak some English. There are private clinics with English-speaking doctors in Tallinn. EU healthcare privileges apply in Estonia, so travellers from the UK require a European Health Insurance Card (EHIC). However, this only guarantees emergency treatment, not all possible expenses, so you should have good health insurance when visiting Tallinn.

Estonia has a relatively low crime rate. However, tourist attractions, such as the Old Town, are prime hunting grounds for sneak thieves, muggers and pickpockets. Keep pricey mobile phones and camera equipment out of sight as much as possible, and leave expensive jewellery at home. If you have a car, park it in a guarded, well-lit car park. You should not walk the streets alone after dark.

If you are the victim of crime, be patient with the police. Many officers, especially the older ones, are not fluent in English. The police are generally courteous and businesslike, but can be slow in filling out crime report forms.

As a visitor, you are required to carry identification at all times, although it is unlikely that you will be required to produce it except when entering and leaving the country.

OPENING HOURS

Shops generally open 10.00–19.00 Monday to Friday, with early closing on Saturday. Some may open on Sundays in the main tourist areas but most will remain closed. Banks are open 09.00–18.00 Monday to Friday and are generally closed at the weekend. Museum opening hours vary, but are generally longer between May and September.

TOILETS

A triangle pointing down indicates the men's room (or an M or *Meeste*) and a triangle pointing upwards is the women's room. The most central public toilets are to be found in the Old Town. Disabled facilities are available in Town Hall Square. The city also has several Swedish-built automatic WC facilities, which require two 1kr. coins.

CHILDREN

Tallinn, especially the Old Town, is a child-friendly place. As you walk the streets, daydreams of knights in shining armour and great battles fought to capture the castle are almost guaranteed, and with any luck you'll find knights, damsels and jesters wandering around, too. If you're after something more educational, head to **Epping Tower** (ⓐ Laboratooriumi 31 ⓣ 601 3001 ⓦ www.eppingtower.info ⓛ 12.00–17.00 Sat & Sun). Here you can try on chain mail, hold a medieval sword, learn candlemaking and hear stories from medieval experts about the ancient city. The Energy Centre (see page 52) boasts oodles of interactive exhibits, computer classes and lightning demonstrations.

Locals also love to take their children to the zoo. **Tallinn Zoo** (ⓐ Paldiski mnt. 145 ⓣ 694 3300 ⓦ www.tallinnzoo.ee ⓛ 09.00–19.00 summer; 09.00–15.00 winter), established in 1939, is home to over

5,000 animals representing nearly 350 species. Kids will love the petting zoo filled with rabbits, hamsters and other small, child-friendly animals.

For entertainment, try the **Estonian Puppet Theatre** (ⓐ Lai 1 ⓣ 667 9555 ⓦ www.nukuteater.ee ⓛ 10.00–18.00), which is suitable for children of all ages.

Children are also quite welcome at some of the more serious places such as concert halls. However, it might be best to select balcony seats in case you need to make a quick getaway at any point. Most restaurants and cafés happily serve children, and some even have a special menu. Estonians are so tolerant of children you may discover the chef is willing to make something special to appease a little appetite. When it comes to getting around, children under the age of seven ride for free on Tallinn's public transport system. Need a taxi large enough to accommodate a pram or pushchair? Advise the dispatcher and you'll be sent a car large enough to suit your needs. Most department stores such as Stockmann and Kaubamaja have nappy-changing facilities. First aid is available at the **Tallinn Children's Hospital** (ⓐ Tervise 28 ⓣ 697 7113).

COMMUNICATIONS
Internet
Tallinn is well served by internet cafés, which is not surprising given the high level of use by its citizens. The cost is about 40–60kr. for an hour. Internet access is also available in public libraries, but there can be a waiting time to get on a terminal.

Tallinn is one of the world's first cities to offer free Wi-Fi access on almost every corner – even garages have it. If you're travelling with your laptop, visit ⓦ www.wifi.ee for the current list of hotspot locations. Many are free, and some offer access for a nominal charge.

Plans are also being drawn up to offer free Wi-Fi on all public transport in Tallinn.

Public access to the internet is offered in the following locations:

@punkt ⓐ Kaubamaja Gonsiori 2, 5th floor ⓦ www.kaubamaja.ee

Apollo Raamatumaja ⓐ Viru 23

Café Espresso ⓐ Estonia pst. 7

Café Sookoll ⓐ Soo 42

Central Library ⓐ Estonia pst. 8 ⓦ www.nlib.ee

Central Post Office ⓐ Narva mnt. 1

Mustamäe Shopping Centre ⓐ Tammsaare tee 116

Stockmann Department Store ⓐ Liivalaia 53

WW Passaazh ⓐ Aia 3

⬤ *Signs in English make orientation in the city easier*

Phone

The telephone system in Estonia is reliable and easy to use. Fixed line numbers within the country have seven digits and there are no area codes. Tallinn has a good supply of public telephone boxes, but they use magnetic cards and not coins. The public phones offer international direct dialling and many have English-language instructions posted inside. If you will be making calls from pay phones, you can purchase cards in denominations of 50 and 100kr. These are available from post offices, newspaper and tobacco kiosks, some supermarkets and the tourist information office.

If you have a GSM mobile phone, it is possible to avoid heavy roaming charges by purchasing a prepaid SIM card from one of the local services, such as EMT Simpel or Tele2 Smart. Starter packs and refills are available at newspaper kiosks.

TELEPHONING ESTONIA

To call anywhere in Estonia, simply dial your country's international access code (usually 00), followed by Estonia's country code (372), followed by the seven-digit number you require. There are no area codes. If you need to reach an operator, dial 16115.

TELEPHONING ABROAD

To call abroad from Estonia, dial 00, then the country code, then the area code (dropping the first '0' if there is one), then the local number you require. Country codes are: UK 44; USA & Canada 1; Republic of Ireland 353; South Africa 27; Australia 61; New Zealand 64.

Post

The Estonia postal system is very efficient. The Tallinn Central Post Office is conveniently located at Narva maantee 1, near the city centre. There are also post offices around town. Many post offices have some staff who speak English.

The Central Post Office is open 08.00 to 20.00 weekdays, 09.00 to 17.00 Saturdays, and is closed on Sundays. Other post offices close at 18.00 on weekdays and are also closed on Saturday afternoons and Sundays.

The cost of sending a letter to the rest of Europe is 6.5kr., and to North America and Australia it is 8kr.

Besides normal postal services, post offices can also be used to send and receive faxes, and to use the internet.

Information on postal services is available at ☎ 661 6616 and at ⓦ www.post.ee

ELECTRICITY

The electrical system in Estonia is very reliable. It is 220 volts AC, 50 hertz. The plug is two pin, European style.

TRAVELLERS WITH DISABILITIES

The Baltic States have a long way to go to become truly wheelchair-accessible, or even wheelchair-friendly. Even in the larger cities, access to public transport and tourist attractions is lacking. The spa resorts (see page 136) and their accommodation and restaurant facilities often have good access for wheelchair users and visitors with other disabilities.

Tourist offices can be especially helpful in determining if there is suitable accommodation in the area you wish to visit if you make your request in advance. The **Tallinn Tourist Office** website (W www.tourism.tallinn.ee) has a very useful section with listings of hotels in the city with at least one wheelchair-accessible guest room and details of accessible restaurants and attractions; click on 'Be Prepared', then 'Accessible Tourism'. It's a good idea to double-check any information you receive, since some establishments will advertise services that are still to be implemented.

If you travel with a wheelchair, have it serviced before your departure and carry any essential parts you may need to do repairs. It is also a good idea to travel with any spares of special clothing or equipment that might be difficult to replace.

Associations dealing with your particular disability can be excellent sources of information on conditions and circumstances in other countries. The following contacts may be helpful:

United Kingdom & Ireland

DPTAC a Zone 4/24, Great Minister House, 76 Marsham Street, London SW1P 4DR, UK t 020 7944 8011 W www.dptac.gov.uk
Irish Wheelchair Association a Blackheath Drive, Clontarf, Dublin 3, Ireland t 01/818 6400 W www.iwa.ie

USA & Canada

Society for Accessible Travel & Hospitality (SATH) a 347 5th Avenue, New York, NY 10016, USA t 212/447-7284 W www.sath.org
Access-Able W www.access-able.com

Australia & New Zealand

National Disability Services Limited (formerly ACROD)
a Locked Bag 3002, Deakin West Act 2600, Australia
t 02/6283 3200 W www.nds.org.au

Disabled Persons Assembly 📧 4/173–175 Victoria Street, Wellington, New Zealand 📞 04/801 9100 🌐 www.dpa.org.nz

TOURIST INFORMATION
Estonian Tourist Board 🌐 www.visitestonia.com
Pärnu Tourist Board 🌐 www.parnu.ee
Tallinn City Tourist Office 🌐 www.tourism.tallinn.ee
Tartu Tourist Office 🌐 www.tartu.ee

BACKGROUND READING
Architecture and Art Movements in Tallinn by Sulev Mäeväli. This readable, informative guide to the city's architectural supermodels broadens out into a valuable cultural companion.
The Baltic States: The Years of Dependence 1940–1990 by Romuald J Misiunas and Rein Taagepera. A study of the effects of occupation that's all the more effective for its calm examination of some horrifying facts.
Tallinn Through the Ages by Raimo Pullat. A charming, anecdotal journey through the city's eventful life.

Emergencies

The following are all national toll-free emergency numbers:
Ambulance ☎ 112
Fire ☎ 112
Police ☎ 110

MEDICAL SERVICES
For entry into Estonia, it is advisable (but not mandatory) to have
a valid health insurance policy. No vaccinations or health certificates
are required. In case of accident or serious illness, call ☎ 112

Pharmacies (*Apteek*) are usually open from 10.00–19.00, but one
stays open all night (☎ Tõnismäe apteek, Tõnismägi 5 ☎ 644 2282).
Ordinary medication is available in all pharmacies.

POLICE
The Estonian police force (*politsei*) was established in 1991.
Officers wear dark blue uniforms, and have special uniforms
for festive occasions.

EMBASSIES & CONSULATES
Australian Consulate ☎ Marja 9, Tallinn ☎ 650 9308
Canadian Embassy ☎ Toom-Kooli 13, 10130 Tallinn ☎ 627 3311
Republic of Ireland Embassy ☎ Vene 2, 10123 Tallinn ☎ 681 1888
South Africa Representation ☎ Rahapajankatu 1 A 5 00160, Helsinki,
Finland ⓦ www.southafricanembassy.fi
UK Embassy ☎ Wismari 6, 10136 Tallinn ☎ 667 4700
ⓦ www.britishembassy.ee
USA Embassy ☎ Kentmanni 20, 15099 Tallinn ☎ 668 8100
ⓦ www.usemb.ee

⬤ *Estonia's finest on patrol in the Old Town*

EMERGENCY PHRASES

Help!	**Fire!**	**Stop!**
Appi!	Põleb!	Stopp!
Ap-pi!	*Poleb!*	*Stop!*

Call an ambulance/a doctor/the police/the fire service!
Kutsuge kiirabi/arst/politsei/tuletõrje!
Kyut-su-keh keer-ah-bi/arst/po-lit-sey/tu-leh-tor-ye!

Editorial/project management: Lisa Plumridge
Copy editor: Monica Guy
Layout/DTP: Alison Rayner

The publishers would like to thank the following individuals and organisations for supplying their copyright photographs for this book: Ann Carroll Burgess, pages 25 & 82; Tom Burgess, pages 5 & 71; Cornelius, page 143; Scott Diel, pages 98, 99 & 127; Dreamstime.com (Allein, page 55; Pontus Edenberg, page 141; Taylor Jackson, page 33; Kokodrill, page 119; Maigi, page 17; Kutt Niinepuu, page 38); Ed G, page 155; Tavi Grepp/Tallinn Tourism, pages 20, 23, 77 & 91; Kaido Haagen/Tallinn Tourism, pages 29 & 97; David Harding/Fotolia, pages 104–5; Imrek/Fotolia, page 41; iStockphoto.com (Adrian Beesley, page 65; Christian Champagne, page 19; emily2k, page 137;

Send your thoughts to
books@thomascook.com

- **Found a great bar, club, shop or must-see sight that we don't feature?**
- **Like to tip us off about any information that needs a little updating?**
- **Want to tell us what you love about this handy little guidebook and more importantly how we can make it even handier?**

Then here's your chance to tell all! Send us ideas, discoveries and recommendations today and then look out for your valuable input in the next edition of this title.

Email the above address (stating the title) or write to:
pocket guides Series Editor, Thomas Cook Publishing, PO Box 227, Coningsby Road, Peterborough PE3 8SB, UK.

WHAT'S IN YOUR GUIDEBOOK?

Independent authors Impartial up-to-date information from our travel experts who meticulously source local knowledge.

Experience Thomas Cook's 165 years in the travel industry and guidebook publishing enriches every word with expertise you can trust.

Travel know-how Thomas Cook has thousands of staff working around the globe, all living and breathing travel.

Editors Travel-publishing professionals, pulling everything together to craft a perfect blend of words, pictures, maps and design.

You, the traveller We deliver a practical, no-nonsense approach to information, geared to how you really use it.

Tomaz Levstek, page 53; Marek Slusarczyk, page 62; Peeter Viisimaa, page 78; Laura Young, page 72); Leo-setä, page 95; Meelis Lokk/ Tartu.ee, page 131; Siyad Ma, pages 101 & 111; neoroma, page 35; SXC.hu (Stefanie Leuker, pages 14–15; Enrico Corno, page 149); Mats Tooming/BigStockPhoto.com, pages 116–17 & 123; Tiit Veermäe/ Hotel Telegraaf, page 42; Toomas Volmer/Tallinn Tourism, pages 7, 9, 11, 44–5, 51, 67 & 89.

Useful phrases

English	Estonian	*Approx pronunciation*
BASICS		
Yes	Jah (jaa)	*Yah (ya-a)*
No	Ei	*A*
Please	Palun	*Pah-loon*
Thank you	Tänan (Aitäh)	*Ta-nan (Ay-tahh)*
Hello	Tere, tervist	*Teh-reh/ter-vist*
Goodbye	Nägemiseni (head aega)	*Na-ghe-mi-seh-ni (he-ad a-e-ga)*
Excuse me	Vabandage	*Vah-ban-da-gheh*
Sorry	Andke andeks	*And-keh and-eks*
That's okay	See sobib	*See sobib*
I don't speak Estonian	Ma ei oska eesti keelt	*Mah ey os-kah e-es-ti ke-elt*
Do you speak English?	Kas te räägite/ oskate inglise keelt?	*Kas te rae-aeghi-te/ os-ka-te ing-li-seh ke-elt?*
Good morning	Tere hommikut	*Teh-reh hom-mi-kuht*
Good afternoon	Tere päevast	*Teh-reh pae-vahst*
Good evening	Tere õhtust	*Teh-reh oh-tuhst*
Goodnight	Head ööd	*He-ad urd*
My name is ...	Minu nimi on. . .	*Minu nimi on...*
NUMBERS		
One	Üks	*Yuks*
Two	Kaks	*Kaks*
Three	Kolm	*Kolm*
Four	Neli	*Neli*
Five	Viis	*Vees*
Six	Kuus	*Coos*
Seven	Seitse	*Seyt-seh*
Eight	Kaheksa	*Kah-hek-sah*
Nine	Üheksa	*Yuh-hek-sah*
Ten	Kümme	*Kym-meh*
Twenty	Kakskümmend	*Kaks-kym-mend*
Fifty	Viiskümmend	*Vees-kyum-mend*
One hundred	Sada	*Sah-da*
SIGNS & NOTICES		
Airport	Lennujaam	*Len-nuh-jahm*
Rail station/Platform	Raudteejaam/Platvorm	*Rowd-te-eh-ya-am/Plat-form*
Smoking/ Non-smoking	Suitsetajatele/ Mittesuitsetajatele	*Suyt-seh-tah-yah-the-leh/Mit-teh-suyt-seh-tah-yah-the-leh*
Toilets	WC (Tualettruum)	*Veh-tseh (Tu-a-lett-room)*
Ladies/Gentlemen	Naistele/Meestele	*Nays-the-leh/Me-es-teh-leh*
Tram	Tramm	*Trah-um*